One
Thousand
Showers

One Thousand Showers

A University Immersed in a Culture of Retaliation and an Avalanche of Lies

A true story

by

Terri Patraw

with

Kathleen Keithley

First edition: June 2013

ISBN-13: 978-0615817798
ISBN-10: 0615817793

Cover Photo by John Byrne

CONTENTS

Dedication

*This book is dedicated to the memory of
Police Sergeant Lane Grow
and
Nevada soccer player Natalie Ratnavira*

FOREWORD

One Thousand Showers

I was a successful NCAA Division I soccer coach who was a champion for her athletes; who embodied everything the NCAA is said to be about. When I reported wrongdoing of a fellow coach my world was turned upside down by a culture of retaliation that engulfed an entire college campus. The recent scandals at Penn State and Rutgers show the harm that a university administration, drunk with power, can cause to individuals and even to the institution itself.

Despite my journalism background, the last thing I ever envisioned was writing a book. Journalism involves short, quick stories. This is a long painful story about subject matter that is so far removed from anything I ever thought about or involved myself in. I loathe politics. I rarely watch the news. Retaliation to me was something that happened on the playing field. It was a bad response to a hard foul. I did not want to write this book. But the never-ending and destructive actions of the university administration gave me no choice.

It can be a risk when you tell the truth, the whole truth. But in the scheme of things and when all is said and done, it's a bigger risk not to tell the truth. Lies and deception have a way of festering within and poisoning your soul and destroying your spirit. Some will admire me for writing this book and others will resent me. Either way, the response of others is not a reflection of me, but rather a reflection of the individual and his or her own moral compass. I'm turning the mirror on them and daring them to take a look.

Through my legal pursuits and all the accompanying aspects of my ordeal, I often said that one thousand showers would not cleanse me of the filth I endured while living and working in Nevada.

I look at this book as my *one thousand and first* shower.

Terri Patraw

CHAPTER 1

Down the Rabbit Hole

"I can honestly say I never had a coach that was more committed or cared about her athletes more than you. You always fought for us . . . . You gave me so much confidence as a player and taught me so much about being a person . . ."
~ Nevada student-athlete

It was the middle of preseason practice, two weeks into the 2007 season and four days before our home opener, when my world was forever changed. I was a highly successful NCAA Division I soccer coach with a master's degree in business administration. My team was coming off a championship season in 2006, winning the conference tournament and earning the university soccer program's first-ever NCAA Tournament bid. My 2007 team had just been voted by our conference peers as the favorite to win the conference. I was at the top of my game.

But things would soon change. I was about to take quite a tumble down the rabbit hole.

* * *

I was the University of Nevada's "superstar" coach, according to a university administrator, having brought the soccer program from cellar dweller to a top echelon program, winning a championship and national acclaim along the way. I was told over and over again by student-athletes, colleagues, the athletic director and the university administration that

I was just what the school needed. The NCAA had even named my program the "Most Improved Team in the Nation."

But then the AD told me that my tenure was over?!

I was shocked and confused. It was all so surreal – nightmarish. I had been flung into an upside down world where bad was good and right was wrong. Had I misheard the words coming from the mouth of my boss, Cary Groth, the Athletic Director at the University of Nevada, Reno, as I sat across the table from her in her office on that sunny day in late August of 2007? But since my hearing was just fine, the only other possible answer was that she must have lost her mind. My team was just coming off a championship season – and championships at the University of Nevada were the exception not the rule. And because of my success and years of outstanding personnel evaluations at the university, I had just been offered a raise, a car and a multi-year contract! I was an unmitigated success at the university, an organization that didn't have much to brag about in women's athletics. My team's attractive and aggressive style of play, along with the mounting victories during my three seasons as head coach, brought in fans who finally had something to cheer about. I was showered with praise from the university president, glowing accolades from Groth herself, congrats from my peers, and thanks from my students, parents and enthusiastic fans.

I replayed the scene in my mind as I stared at Groth in disbelief. Minutes before everything seemed sane, when I nonchalantly walked in her office ready to finalize the negotiation of the raise and multi-year contract extension she had offered me just six days earlier.

But it hadn't gone quite that way.

"Terri, you're a great, great coach. Nobody can deny that. I just need to move on. I looked in your personnel file. There was nothing to use against you," Groth had said.

Groth confirmed what I already knew. She told me in the presence of Gena Jones, Assistant Vice President of Human Resources, that she was ending my tenure without cause. Now it was all out in the open and we were in agreement. She *confessed* that her grounds were baseless.

So, again, why was she doing this?

But then it occurred to me. I had recently reported serious improprieties of a fellow coach to my supervisor. I had done so to protect the athletic program, the student-athletes, and the university. I took my job seriously and I had done the only responsible thing I could have done.

But it hadn't gone any further than Groth. It was totally manageable and I had not gone outside the athletic administration. I did hear in the interim that Groth was particularly close to this coach – something that should not have mattered to a professional athletic director – but in this case it had.

When I caught my breath, I asked Groth directly – which is the only way I know how to communicate – *what the hell she was talking about.*

"This has whistleblower retaliation written all over it," I said.

Groth averted her eyes before she responded.

"I know," she surprisingly blurted out.

I KNOW?! She said it! She admitted it just like that. She was retaliating against me because I had informed the administration that a fellow coach was jeopardizing the welfare of the student-athletes and the integrity of the institution. The AD was admitting that she was ending my career at Nevada for improper reasons.

Groth not only told me that she knew there was no basis for her decision; she outright admitted that it was illegal. I was stunned. She had lost her mind. I searched her face to find the hint of a smile, a crack in the façade that would tell me that she was just kidding. Of course, I would not have found her words the least bit amusing under any circumstance. And ribbing me would have been out of character for the very stoic athletic director who had not shown even the semblance of a sense of humor up to that point. But I had to grasp for something to hold onto, something that would diffuse her inexplicable words, explain the unexplainable. But there was nothing, only a deep and incomprehensible abyss that held no real explanation. Bottom line, this woman was serious. I was done – there was no discussion or debate or anything I could say that could change that. That was it.

I walked out of Groth's office feeling angry and betrayed after having been forced to say a quick farewell to my stunned athletes. I said a tearful good-bye to them . . . I couldn't remember the last time I had cried before that moment. As I walked away from the people and program that had come to mean so much to me in my life, I thought, okay, Cary Groth, you cannot possibly believe that I am going to just roll over and walk away from this?! I am not handing over my successful career to you. I am a United States Soccer Federation National "A" licensed coach, and an extremely successful Division I soccer coach and recruiter with the requisite aggressive, scrappy personality that goes with it. I didn't take a loss lying down, sitting down, or even standing up.

Eventually, Groth and others including the Nevada System of Higher Education (NSHE), the UNR legal team and the band of mercenary attorneys that they over time amassed against me, the local media, the entire Nevada judicial system and ultimately even the NCAA would learn that I was a fighter, a winner, and not one to be intimidated.

I had learned to play by the rules from one of my heroes and I had learned to fight and survive from another.

Initially I was, of course, shocked but when the shock gave way to anger – and I have always been able to parlay my anger to wind up in a better place – the question lingered: how could this have happened?! That day when I was unexpectedly sidelined by my AD was one of the few moments when my life skipped a beat, when I felt lost and abandoned and defeated. That said, it was a short-term condition, a very short-term condition – in fact, it had already begun to fade by the time I got to my car. Although my positive glass-is-half-full attitude that I had enjoyed my entire life was drained, it soon began to replenish itself. Before I drove off from the university, I had decided that I would fight this ridiculous turn of events. I would get my job back.

*   *   *

Anyone who encourages their kids or students to participate in college athletics and those young athletes who may consider a career in coaching or professional sports need to read my story carefully. I love soccer and sports. It's part of me. It's in my DNA. Some people have soothing background music playing while they work . . . ESPN's SportsCenter or whatever game is taking place at the time is my background music. Its tempo is in sync with my soul.

If this outrageous injustice can happen to me, a fighter who played by the rules, it can happen to anyone.

As you read my story, I ask you to remember two things. First, I was dedicated to my job and my student-athletes at Nevada. I LOVED the soccer program that I had developed at the university and I did everything that I could to PROTECT the institution and its fragile athletic program. What I placed above everything else, however, were my student-athletes and I threw myself completely into supporting them in achieving their goals and successes, encouraging them to believe in themselves and their abilities and helping them to recognize the full spectrum of possibilities that lay before them with every bit of energy I could muster and everything that I had in me. I wasn't betrayed by my students or by the sport I love; I was betrayed by corruption that is widespread and pervasive and that touched most of the major segments of the Reno, Nevada, community.

It is that corrupt system that I am calling out with this book. A lot has been misrepresented about me in the press and in open court. Let me retract that. What I just said was way too nice. I was blatantly lied about, conspired against and my reputation was smeared by corrupt, unsavory and untrustworthy people in positions of trust and power who didn't possess the fundamental character necessary to hold them.

This book is my chance to tell my story, the true story.

This book is my justice.

The second thing that I ask you to keep in mind is that I was a victim of this corruption but I've never been "the victim" before. I don't play one well and don't care to be one. Pulling on the "victim" costume was an impossible task for me. Being the target of this outrage was something that I didn't want or expect but it was something that I couldn't avoid. And the venom that fueled the lies was something that I wasn't about to shrink away from.

Let me tell you about myself and my background in the briefest terms possible and how it relates to this story. And then allow me to tell you the entire story of what happened to me in Nevada. What happens in Vegas reportedly stays in Vegas. But what happened to me in Reno followed me, haunted me like a tortured spirit that would not rest until the truth was out.

*   *   *

I was born and raised in Shoreview, Minnesota, a middle class suburb of Minneapolis-St. Paul and home to many of Minnesota's 10,000 lakes. I grew up in the culture of "Minnesota Nice" and am the youngest of three sisters and have one younger brother. We all played soccer practically from the time we could walk. I'm sure we all came into life literally ready to kick a soccer ball! My parents were always involved in our sports. I cannot remember a game they missed throughout our childhood. My dad often coached our teams – sports and coaching were always part of our family, part of our world. My nephews and nieces have continued the tradition and all play on youth soccer teams. One of my sisters and my brother both coach their kids' teams today.

From my earliest memories, I always loved everything about sports, both competing in them and as a fan. I played soccer, basketball, and softball throughout my childhood. At eight years of age, I knew that I was really good at soccer. I never lacked for confidence on the soccer field and was never shy or reserved about outplaying the boys – which I did most of the time – or playing up several age groups to be on my sisters' teams.

I was innately competitive and as I played sports through the years I naturally wanted to win. But winning wasn't everything to me – it was *very* important but being raised in a relatively large family taught me the value and meaning of teamwork. It wasn't important that I won; it was important that the team won and that I did everything to the best of my abilities to make that happen.

I learned the rules of the game when I was young and they became part of my fiber. My father and I had so much in common. Our minds were always on sports. I hung out on the couch with Dad in the family room watching all the games – football, basketball, hockey, soccer – and then analyzing why a team won or lost. I loved him as my dad and I admired and respected his passion for sports. My dad is a rule follower and a law-abiding man. We were raised on the principles of hard work and responsibility. It is therefore not a surprise that all of my siblings have also gone onto successful professional careers.

My dad was my sports hero but my mother was my real life hero. At five-feet two inches in height, it was rare that I had the opportunity to look down on someone in stature – with my mother being the sole exception. While my mother is a shade or two under five-feet tall, *nobody* dared look down on her! My mother may have been exaggerating a bit if she said she was five-feet tall but she always was and remains a powerhouse and real force in my life. She was brave in the face of personal tragedy and was always there for all four of us kids. She beat cancer twice, most recently just in 2011. Her family still needed her and she wasn't about to leave us. She wasn't going to let a little cancer get in the way. She's a spitfire and while my father taught me the rules of the game, my mother inspired me to be a fighter and a survivor. I could not have survived what happened to me in Nevada if it hadn't been for her.

Along the way I gained other heroes one of which was the *National Collegiate Athletic Association.* I admired the force of fairness that the NCAA represented in the sports I loved. They literally created the level playing field. They were the watchdog group to make sure there was no discrimination and that everyone in university level sports was playing by the same rules. Athletes of all stripes were viewed the same by the NCAA – men, women, average players and superstars. The NCAA showed no prejudice or bias and allowed no student-athlete to have an unfair advantage or to be mistreated among the sports programs of the nation's institutions of higher learning. As a high school female interested in intercollegiate athletics, I was quite impressed by the tenets of the NCAA and felt the confidence and comfort that if I chose to participate as a student-athlete in college or someday elected to pursue a coaching position at the university level, my gender would not be an obstacle.

I had been playing on youth soccer teams since I was little so by the time I got to middle school, I was quite a veteran. I was born with the natural aggressiveness thanks to Mom and learned the importance of teamwork from my father. I had no problem in the classroom and although I did fine, I could have done better. My B's could have been A's and my C's could have been B's. But I didn't lose any sleep over it. My future would not be in the classroom. It would be on the playing field. I found my niche early unlike some kids who don't have a clue as to who they are or what they want to become when they arrive at college. I attribute my early ability to self-identify to both my parents who always allowed me to be who I was. As a coach, I applied that same philosophy in working with my student-athletes, which proved to be the key in getting the best out of each individual athlete.

I was inducted into the Mounds View High School Hall of Fame and was honored by the City of Shoreview for my "Dedication and Sportsmanship." As a high school senior, I had the temerity to tell a local reporter that I would earn a Division I soccer scholarship at the University of Wisconsin-Madison and major in journalism. As it turned out, that is exactly what happened. I had thoughts about having a career as a sports reporter, writing and filing reports and editorials on sports figures and events. Of course, I never imagined I would be writing a book about my own career in sports. Despite initially toying with the idea of sports reporting, my plans of a career in journalism gave way to a bigger dream and my true love – coaching soccer.

I had an amazing collegiate student-athlete experience, playing in the Final Four and on a team that was ranked #2 in the nation. Individually, I was named a Central Region All-American and was selected to participate in two United States Olympic Sports Festivals.

Throughout my playing career, I had the opportunity to play with and against some of the best players in the world, many who were destined to become household names. While playing for the Wisconsin Badgers, I competed against nine members of the 1999 United States World Cup Team – the team that won the World Cup and stole the heart of America. These US women captured the imagination of the nation in their championship win at the sold-out Rose Bowl in Los Angeles. No one will forget Brandi Chastain's sports bra celebration that made the cover of *Sports Illustrated.*

Some of the nascent stars that I had the privilege of competing against included Mia Hamm, Kristine Lilly, Carla Overbeck all of the University of North Carolina. I took the field against Michelle Akers of the University of Central Florida. Michelle went on to be named the FIFA Player of the Century in 2000 and is arguably the best woman who ever played the game. Michelle was also a teammate of mine at the US Olympic Festival. As a kid I played against Briana Scurry at home in Minnesota and faced her later when she played for the University of Massachusetts. Joy Fawcett of California-Berkeley and Shannon McMillan and Tiffeny Milbrett, both of the University of Portland, were some of my competitors who went on to become stars of the game. And one of my most memorable matches was against Julie Foudy of Stanford, who is a current analyst and color commentator for ESPN.

My time at Wisconsin helped to shape my coaching style and gave me the foundation and credentials to be the highly successful coach and recruiter at the NCAA Division I level that I ultimately became.

After coaching several high school teams in Madison during my college years, I earned a coaching staff position with the Region II Olympic Development program where I trained and identified top youth players in the Midwest Region for the US Soccer Federation. That opportunity opened doors for me at the NCAA Division I level. From there, I held assistant coach/recruiting coordinator positions with both the University of Kentucky and Washington State University. At both universities I was able to impact their programs and student-athletes positively while learning under veteran head coaches. During the offseason at Kentucky,

I would sneak into the gym and watch the basketball team practice whenever the opportunity allowed. An avid basketball fan, I admired watching Head Coach Rick Pitino and his staff – which included a young assistant named Billy Donovan – develop their team and their aggressive, pressing style of play; a style my teams would later emulate on the soccer field.

It was at Arizona State University in Tempe, Arizona, that I was hired for my first head coaching position. I was able to build the university's NCAA Division I soccer program from its inception to a #13 national ranking among a total of 277 programs, accomplishing this in only four recruiting classes. During my five-year tenure as ASU's head coach, the program developed into one of the nation's elite.

My recruiting efforts yielded several nationally ranked recruiting classes including a top ten for 2001. Three of my student-athletes participated on the US Women's national team, and even more went on to secure roster spots on professional teams. Amy LePeilbet, a starting defender for the US Olympic Team that won the gold medal in 2012, possesses the most distinguished post-collegiate soccer career in ASU history. I also recruited and coached All-American Stacey Tullock – ASU's all-time leading scorer – who earned Pac-10 Freshman of the Year and Pac-10 Player of the Year honors. She led the conference in scoring in both her freshman and sophomore years and was also a finalist for National Player-of-the-Year. Through tremendous effort and some creativity, I was successful in recruiting some of the top high-school players in the nation to ASU.

The level of play in which my team participated was epitomized by the caliber of teams it competed against. One of my fondest memories from ASU was a game against the University of Washington in 2000. We lost a 1-0 heartbreaker in what was nothing short of a fantastic game between two very talented and evenly matched teams. A sophomore named Hope Solo defended the nets for Washington, earning the shutout. Based on her performance that day, it came as no surprise when she went on to become the starting goalkeeper for the US National Team and a two-time Olympic gold medalist (2008 and 2012).

Throughout my coaching tenure at Arizona State, I had a growing desire to earn my master's degree in business administration. Having spent seven days a week and too many nights in the office well past midnight in building the ASU soccer program in the rugged Pac Ten Conference,

I resigned my position in January of 2001, and moved across campus to complete my M.B.A. with an eye toward securing my future in athletic administration. While working on my M.B.A., I established a real estate investment company – Patraw Investments, LLC, in Scottsdale, Arizona. But, coaching never left my blood. I found myself sitting in class trying to apply business organizational strategies to a collegiate soccer program. At ASU I had established a great program and highly effective recruiting strategies based on hard work and determination. As a young head coach in a premier conference, I grew tremendously over the years amassing victories and developing positive relationships with administrators and peers and, most importantly, with my student-athletes and their families. My experience at ASU was both satisfying and successful. My positive performance evaluations confirmed my growth and continued success from one year to the next.

> *I just wanted to say thanks for all that you've done for me. From my freshman year until now I have learned so much and you have been my guide . . . You have done so much for the team and have definitely made my stay here [at ASU] most memorable. The team will definitely miss all your hard work and dedication you put in the program . . . Anyone would be more than pleased to have you working for them!*
>
> *Love,*
> *Jaclyn Clark, 12-13-00*

An overview of my career reflected a background that encompassed NCAA Division I athletic programs in the Pac Ten, SEC, and Big Ten conferences. Upon completion of my M.B.A., I was more than qualified and prepared to take on another challenge. I applied for the first two Division I head coaching positions available that offseason – the University of Nevada and Colorado College. I landed interviews at both schools just days apart. The University of Nevada was looking for a dynamic coach who could pump life into the women's soccer team that was ranked in the bottom of NCAA Division I teams since its inception five years earlier.

I brought an energy and enthusiasm to the University of Nevada that was impossible to destroy . . . but in the end they tried their level best to do just that.

CHAPTER 2

The New Head Coach

"The only place success comes before work is in the dictionary."

~ Vince Lombardi

During the two-day interview process at Nevada, I met with staff members of Nevada's athletic department, both individually and in groups. After the interview concluded, my final meeting was with Cindy Fox, who was the Associate Athletic Director at Nevada. I was really impressed with Cindy. She had a dynamic, energetic personality, and, like me, she had previously worked in high profile athletic departments. We really clicked and she was someone I felt I would enjoy working for. I felt satisfied that the entire process had gone well and that I had a good chance of being selected for the position. Two days after I returned home from Nevada, I wrote to Cindy, thanking her for the opportunity to interview and offering her full access to my ASU personnel file. I wanted Cindy to be assured that my on-field success at ASU was supported by my supervisors' evaluations of me.

Less than two weeks later, I got the word from Nevada. I was being offered the head coaching position for their soccer program. According to Cindy, I was the unanimous choice of the hiring committee. I had been interviewing with Colorado College as well but Nevada offered first and I accepted. I was pleased that they offered me first because it was the position that I preferred. I was a proven program builder and I felt that I could breathe new life into Nevada's program. It simply felt like a better fit for me than Colorado College.

I was thrilled to get back into coaching again. While I had felt good about my decision to take time off while earning my MBA, coaching was where I belonged. At ASU, I had taken on the challenge of developing an NCAA Division I soccer program from the ground up. Nevada would be a different challenge. I'd have to turn a program around that was floundering at the bottom of the conference, and was statistically one of the worst Division I programs in the nation. I particularly wanted the spot at Nevada because I knew I could make a difference there. They needed a coach who knew the game, who had the know-how to develop a viable and successful program and who would genuinely care about the student-athletes. The team needed new life and I was filled with the requisite energy, experience and enthusiasm that could supply a fresh start. I was more than ready to take on that challenge after sitting in the classroom for two and a half years, and I was confident that I could make the program a success. I didn't have a single doubt that I could develop a championship team there.

The hiring process at Nevada was slightly unconventional in that I was officially hired by the Associate Athletic Director, Cindy Fox. Nevada was in the process of hiring a new Athletic Director at the time of my hire. The outgoing athletic director had already announced that he was stepping down to return to his previous position at Nevada, as head football coach. The new Nevada Athletic Director, Cary Groth, would be hired approximately two months after my start date. Groth, a former tennis coach, was most recently the Athletic Director at Northern Illinois University, a small Division I school in the Midwest. She had spent her entire professional career at Northern Illinois.

Cindy Fox was a warm and welcoming person and we became fast friends. My initial impression of her was that she was well qualified and capable enough to assume the Athletic Director position. When I learned that her husband, Mark, was Nevada's assistant basketball coach, I understood why she was satisfied with being an associate athletic director. Mark had future designs on becoming the head basketball coach at Nevada and nepotism issues would have interfered with his goals had his wife been named the Athletic Director. And, just two months after Cary Groth was named Nevada's Athletic Director, she named Mark Fox the Head Men's Basketball Coach. With Cindy as associate athletic director and Mark as head basketball coach, the couple held two of the four most powerful positions in Nevada's athletic department – the others, of course, being the athletic director and the football coach.

Cindy was a straightforward woman, just the kind of person to whom I could best relate. We both shared a passion for college sports, and in particular for college basketball. Over the three and a half years I was at Nevada, I would often wind up in her office to talk and discuss how things were going on a business as well as personal basis. She became both a mentor and friend, someone who I trusted and admired. I learned that her husband, Mark, had begun his career at Nevada in an entry level assistant coaching position, working his way up to the head coaching position five years later. Shortly after Cary was hired she gave Cindy a title promotion. Cindy was now the Executive Associate Athletic Director, a newly created title at Nevada.

At Nevada, I felt I had found a home, found a place where I belonged. When I finally settled into the position and became acclimated to my new surroundings, I immediately dug in with energy and enthusiasm. Only then did I realize what a challenge I was actually taking on. There didn't seem to be much overall support for the soccer program at Nevada. I wasn't naïve having been a head coach in Division I sports before and I knew and understood that the men's program – particularly football and basketball – always got the lion's share of support, had the biggest fan base and brought in the revenue to the school. I was optimistic though that the new AD would bring a spirit of renewal and provide a fresh start for the entire athletic department. I laid out my philosophy to my new team at our first meeting – *push, pull or get off.* In other words, move the program forward or get off the bus. No one would be just along for the ride and everyone's contributions would move us forward in a positive direction. I asked my student-athletes to trust me and to follow my lead. I also assured them that we would be the fittest, fastest, and hardest working team in the conference. We would not disappoint.

Upon my first meeting with Cary Groth, I was a little surprised by her almost timid demeanor. She was very laid back and did not show the level of enthusiasm that an AD usually demonstrates. I figured she just had a different approach and that her methods could be as effective and successful as a more aggressive and exuberant AD. Time would tell.

One thing that nagged at me during the entire time I worked under Groth was how unsure of herself she was; I felt she lacked the necessary confidence that was essential for someone in a leadership position to have. Her lack of command wasn't just my imagination. Specifically, I was bothered by an ongoing issue in which Groth's character flaw had negatively manifested itself. For example, each of the sixteen head coaches was issued an annual budget through the Athletic Director's office. We were told by Groth that that was it – we had to make the funds stretch and to use them wisely. Simply put, as head coaches it was our job to manage our budget. I took her at her word and conducted the business and financial part of my responsibilities accordingly. Each year, I operated within my budget, while ensuring my student-athletes the best possible experience. But I learned that I was an exception. It seemed Groth's words didn't have much sway with some of the other coaches. Several coaches went well over-budget. Rather than being held accountable, they instead were rewarded with Groth's approval for additional funds to cover their overages. This inability to hold her subordinates accountable on basic management issues proved to be an overall leadership flaw that ultimately caused tremendous damage to the Nevada athletic program.

When she first came on board, I didn't want to make any snap judgments about her although the gossip mills were already churning. Word had gotten around that at a gathering of Nevada supporters a male donor had asked her an inappropriate personal question about her sexual orientation. My first thought on hearing this was that the donor was completely out of line. A colleague shared with me that Groth's response had been that she was straight. Although I was appalled by the behavior of the donor, I was surprised to hear that Groth was not more forthcoming about herself to an important donor when Reno was such a small town and the truth would be nearly impossible to conceal. Nevada needed to hold onto every donor that it had. Maybe she was concerned about the university or perhaps her ability to raise money from the good-old-boys. The entire episode was small time to me and I didn't think about it again – until much later.

In my three and a half years at Nevada, my relationship with Cary Groth was fine. We weren't close but we had a professional, respectful relationship. In all the time I knew her, I think we had coffee once, played golf once, and only talked at length during my annual evaluations, which were always positive, even glowing. She had no problem with me and I had no problem with her. She also indicated that she was pleased with my performance with occasional notes of support:

Terri,

. . . You have prepared those young so well. They are in great shape and were well coached. I am very proud of you, your coaches and athletes. You deserve this victory Terri . . . .

Cary S. Groth
Director of Athletics
University of Nevada

Terri –

. . . I really am fortunate to work with coaches like you who have the vision it takes to go to the next level. Keep up the great job you are doing . . . .

Cary

Terri –

This note is a great reflection of you – . . . pure class!

Cary

I was doing my job and she recognized it. And because we weren't close on a personal level, I found an incident involving her during my second year there quite strange. I was at a weekend basketball game when she came in and sat with me. Without any prompting, she told me something that shocked me. She disclosed her intention to fire the football coach, Chris Ault. He had been the AD before Groth but left the position when he decided to return to coaching football. He was having a winning season and doing very well by any measure. In fact, he was preparing for a post-season bowl game in Hawaii as we spoke. I wondered to myself if she was trying to provoke a comment from me or if she was looking for confirmation that she was doing the right thing. If so, I didn't bite and remained quiet. First of all, I was stunned that she was telling me something so very personal about a colleague. His job performance wasn't in my purview. Sharing her opinion about one of my colleagues was unprofessional and against any number of HR standards. Secondly, and most jarring to me, I couldn't fathom why she'd want to get rid of a winning coach.

"Winning coach" . . . those words would echo over and over again in my ears a short year later in August 2007 when I, a winning coach, was told that my tenure was over.

*   *   *

I kept in close contact with my family, of course, and always went home for the holidays. Our holidays are not typical by any stretch. Our entire family – parents, kids and grandkids – often go to Jamaica for Christmas. Nearly every year, we exchange the white snow of Minnesota for the white sands of Jamaica in late December and we all agree that it is the perfect swap. My sister and her husband were married in Jamaica one year. It was that event that started the annual Jamaican vacations. I always felt refreshed and renewed after the holidays. And in the 2004-2005 season I needed that lift because I had quite a mountain ahead of me to climb. Bringing my team up to speed wasn't an insurmountable goal by any means. I knew it would be quite a haul but I was up for the challenge.

Bottom line, when I took over the head coaching position at Nevada in 2004, I inherited a team that had never recorded a winning season nor qualified for postseason play. But from day one, I vowed to turn the Nevada soccer program, the Wolf Pack, into a competitive and exciting program – one that would put the school on the NCAA map. In three short years I was able to do just that. Of course, there was a lot of good old-fashioned hard work and dedication and lots of time and energy on the part of me and my coaching staff, and of course the student-athletes, but no one ever complained. We relished the opportunity before us. The student-athletes enjoyed their sport and the challenge of turning the program around. I allowed my assistant coaches a lot of leeway. I wasn't a control freak and knew that the approach that I took in empowering them to coach and deal with the requisite paperwork was good for their future ambitions of becoming head coaches. As for me, I was in my element and I felt fortunate to be there, loving every minute of it.

Despite the support I gave my two young assistant coaches, Graeme and Antoinette – or Nettie as everyone called her – in my third season I sensed that something was amiss. I always believe the best in people until they prove me wrong. This optimistic approach can also prove to be naive. I had reason to believe that Nettie was being disloyal to me. I initially tried to pass it off as professional immaturity. I figured that by giving her significant responsibility within the program, she may have begun to overvalue or misunderstand her role. Based on feedback from colleagues and students she was taking credit for the team's success away from the rest of the coaching staff and the students themselves. To help her grow as a coach and professional, it was something I had to deal with. I had a history with Nettie. She had played for me at Arizona State University. I had known her and her family since she was 17 years old. I understand human nature but drew a line in the sand when it came to my team – I wouldn't allow any issue to linger that could affect the program. It was my duty as the head of the program to deal with this minor issue before it became a major one. I had a conversation with Nettie. I don't know how to play games other than those on the field, so I confronted her directly about it. I told her that I had reason to doubt her loyalty to me and to the program. She denied this and I accepted her response. My point was made. A short while later she returned to my office in tears, clearly hurt by the allegation of disloyalty. I told her that it was all water under the bridge and hoped that my message had been taken to heart. I felt for her because I'd worked with her first as a student-athlete and then as my assistant coach. Looking back on the incident now, I see that I let my loyalty to her override what was a compelling reason to fire her.

Playing by the rules was the only game in town as far as I was concerned even though it was the consensus that the town in question – Reno, Nevada – played by its own rules. I closely adhered to NCAA regulations so I was taken aback when Dan Dugan, an individual in the community who I did not know, contacted me and told me that he and his organization, the Reno Sparks United Soccer Club, a local youth sports organization, were proud to be affiliated with the university soccer program. He expected to continue the special access to university facilities that his club had previously enjoyed. I welcomed him to those games and events at the university that were open to the public but pushed back on his statement that his organization was affiliated with Nevada Wolf Pack Soccer. We were a state university operating under the rules of the NCAA and as such we were not able to show any preference to any private sports organization or individual. I was surprised by his assertion but was even more stunned when I learned that he was the husband of UNR's General Counsel, Mary Dugan. I hadn't met her yet but was perplexed that the husband of the university's head legal counsel would contact me expressing the expectation that favoritism would be shown to his sports club. If I knew it was illegal and against NCAA rules, Mary Dugan certainly did. I later learned that the head coach I had replaced, Coach Dang Pibulvech, was a friend of the Dugans and had been a coach in this club – which included among its players the Dugans' young triplet sons.

According to Cindy Fox, Mary Dugan had been livid over the termination of Dang's employment at the university. That the program had four straight losing seasons apparently wasn't important to her and didn't help convince Dugan that a coaching change was the right move for the program and student-athletes. Because I was Dang's replacement, I was automatically fighting an uphill battle to win favor with the Dugans. I dismissed the entire thing at the time but would eventually learn the hard way that certain people didn't like to be crossed – job performance, rules and regulations be damned.

After my third season, there was an opening for a head soccer coach at Wisconsin, my alma mater. Graeme told me he'd like to go with me if I got that position. I hadn't applied for it nor had I declared any intention to but I asked him if he wouldn't want to stay on with Nettie who could be next in line to take over the head coaching position at Nevada if I were to leave. He said he wouldn't want to work under her. I was a little taken aback. They seemed close and spent a lot of time together socially. I was flattered at his support for me, yet surprised at his consternation about working under Nettie. Perhaps he too saw the professional disloyalty that I was sensing about her. Graeme and I did not spend much time together socially but we did share a love for the golf course and on occasion went golfing together. In fact, one week before my final day at Nevada, Graeme and I spent the day playing golf, talking about the upcoming season and soaking in the hot August sun. In the coming months, I would see up close and personal just how devastating it can be when loyalty is distorted and transforms itself into real venom.

In my second year at Nevada, my friendship with Dedrique, an assistant basketball coach, escalated and we began to date but did so discreetly. Groth had no idea we were ever involved until much later. Dedrique and I thought it best to keep our relationship under the radar although it wasn't against any rules. In fact, the department was lax about personal relationships among staff. Groth's domestic partner was hired as an academic advisor in the athletic department during Groth's tenure as AD. And, of course, Cindy Fox, the Associate AD, was married to Mark Fox, the Head Basketball Coach. My relationship with Dedrique was short-lived, and we worked together several more months before he left for a coaching position at another school. Several years later, I would be very surprised when Dedrique surfaced again and played a role when I was in the fight of my life to get my job back.

*   *   *

When I had assumed the head coaching position in the 2004-2005 season, I knew it was a time of restructuring and development and although it was not a winning season, there were strong and definite signs that things were turning around. Although our losses outnumbered our wins, the improved level of play on the field was significant, and it was applauded by the administration. In 2005, just my second year at the helm, I became Nevada's winningest soccer coach in school history. With the help of my assistants, I guided the Wolf Pack to a program-best record of 11-7-2 and set the school mark with a 4-2-1 conference record, which gained the team second in league standings. The team was named the most improved Division I team in the nation by the NCAA. With just one recruiting class in place, the Wolf Pack racked up eleven victories after turning in a 2-15-1 record in 2004.

I worked with my student-athletes both as a team and as individuals. I instilled a 'no fear of failure' attitude in my athletes and encouraged them to be themselves on and off the field. Everyone had a valuable role on my team. Someone would be the best defender. Someone would be our best student. Someone else would be our fittest player. I coached my students to discover what they were best at and to be amazing at it. I focused on strengths and urged my athletes to just be themselves ever mindful that these were young people who needed leadership and goals to strive for. I was always there for them. One of my players referred to me as their 24/7 coach. And I was just that.

Terri,

It is hard to choose what exactly to say to you or what to thank you for. You do so many things I'm always thinking, "don't forget to thank Terri for that or tell her what it meant to you."

Whether it was a former coach or myself that put me there, I was in a dark place when it came to soccer at this level and in bad shape with an outlook of myself as a player. I truly believe that you helped to salvage what was left of the soccer player inside myself.

You probably hear this sort of thing a lot-which is maybe why others or myself do not say it a lot but, thank you for everything. When I say everything I truly mean that in every sense of the word. For the time, equipment, the way you take care of <u>your</u> players and <u>your</u> team. Your attitude is incredible and I feel privileged to say that I have played under your direction.

Your ability to create success is unbelievable and I feel lucky to be a part.

Thank you,
Nevada student-athlete

Throughout my tenure at Nevada, my staff and I put a lot of time and energy into recruiting. Through hard work and determination we were able to bring in some of the best female student-athletes not only from the US but from across the globe. In my three recruiting classes at Nevada, we signed four Australians and one Canadian, along with a number of US players from several different states. During the 2006-07 season, we continued to shatter program records both individually and collectively as a team. We finished the season with a 13-5-4 record, while outscoring our opponents an astounding 43-14! Boasting the conference's leading goal scorer, we led the league in every offensive category. Our goalkeeper anchored our stellar defense and was named Conference Tournament MVP. We won the first conference championship in program history and earned a bid to the NCAA Tournament. That too was a first. On the heels of the program's success, I was honored as a Regional Coach of the Year Finalist.

Terri,

. . . I just feel that I owe you too much at this point to leave things unsaid. So I want to try to tell you how much I have appreciated what you have done for me and for this team, even if the words don't come out just right . . .

. . . The Washington State game was nothing short of brilliant. It really didn't matter what other team was out on the field because on that day, we were perfect. And while I wish I had more time to spend with you guys, I am so grateful that I came when I did. To know where this program had been in the past and to witness a performance like that was incredible. I do not believe that I ever could have truly appreciated a year like we just had with my prior experiences here. I would never have wanted it as badly, it could never have meant so much to me as it does right now.

Most of these girls don't even know how lucky they are and how great of an opportunity they finally have here. This program bears no resemblance to the struggling team I committed to years ago and as long as you are here, I am confident it will never resemble such again. They are going to be brilliant. You are going to be brilliant. As far as I'm concerned, you guys already are.

I am always going to remember seeing your car parked outside of Legacy Hall. It didn't matter the day or hour, it always seemed to be there without fail. You always seemed to be there without fail. Words like driven, dedicated, and determined don't even begin to describe what you are. I have never witnessed such belief, that which radiates and anyone near it can't help but comply. Nor have I known anyone more willing to give up so much for the benefit of so many. Your conviction speaks lengths, but its effects shall remain immeasurable.

I do want to thank you for allowing me to be a part of this program. More than that though, I want to thank you for making this program something worth being a part of. To get to share my time here with such amazing individuals who so willingly commit their lives to one another. I am truly blessed to have such people in my life. The best decision I ever made was deciding to play soccer for the University of Nevada I could not have said that two years ago. I know that none of this would have been possible if you had not come here. I don't know how you can ever really thank anyone for something like that, something that big. And while I don't ever expect for you to understand the depth of my gratitude, I do hope that you know that it has meant everything to me.

You're coach of the year in my book! I truly cannot thank you enough. And, Terri, you've still got it . . . you always will.

Take care of you,
Megan Tarpenning – "Tarp"

After earning another stellar personnel evaluation from Cindy, Cary, and the university president, and receiving my third straight annual merit raise that off-season, I was looking forward to the 2007-2008 season. I would put all my efforts into keeping my team in top form and performing at our personal best. I had an offer for another raise and a multi-year extension on the table. Everything was looking up. It had been hard work but it was paying off for the school, for me personally and mainly for my student-athletes.

I looked forward to the new year like never before.

CHAPTER 3

An Upside Down World

"When something bad happens to you, you have three choices. You can either let it define you, let it destroy you, or you can let it strengthen you."

~ Author Unknown

Of course, the 2007-2008 season at Nevada didn't happen for me. It all ended in late August 2007 and I was devastated.

Our team had just been selected by our conference peers in a pre-season poll as THE team to win the conference in 2007. We had won the conference tournament in 2006, which earned us a bid to the NCAA Tournament, where we lost 2-1 to a great Stanford team. We had brought in another stellar recruiting class that off-season, our third straight class that was ranked #1 in our conference by *Soccer Buzz Magazine*. Our expectations were high, and we were set to build on the success of the previous season. We were in the middle of preseason practice, just two weeks into the 2007 season and four days away from our home opener when I was set back on my heels and my world was turned upside down.

I went golfing with my assistant coach Graeme Abel about a week before all hell broke loose. I had a good relationship with my assistants and allowed them to grow and flourish but I didn't typically socialize with them. I had brought Graeme in from an NAIA school in Kentucky and gave him his first NCAA Division I job. Similarly, I gave Nettie her first Division I job after her first coaching job at Elmira University, a

Division III school in New York. There had never been any problems other than that little dust-up with Nettie, but that had passed. Graeme and I both loved to play golf and our schedules were closely aligned so we took advantage of it once in a while with a round of golf. Graeme and I had a played eighteen holes that day but neither of us would have dreamed that it would be our last game together. Both of us had red noses and cheeks from being in the sun all afternoon. I was gone before my sunburn faded.

The day before I met with Groth on that final day, the university issued a press release and posted it on their website praising me and the soccer program's outstanding growth under my leadership. Talk about job security. How many employees have an "atta boy" press release issued about their performance? Why would I think there was anything to worry about? Exceptional personnel evaluations, annual merit raises, winning program, and a multi-year contract offer on the table!

The very next day, after Cary Groth gave me the unexpected news that my career at Nevada was over, I was reeling. My mind was spinning. My life had just been shaken *and* stirred and turned upside down and I was struggling to find my footing, to grasp this new reality that had been forced upon me. I felt as though I was being buried alive. As the shovels full of dirt were being thrown on my face, my voice, inexplicably silenced, I wanted to scream out and say, "Stop! This is all a huge mistake. I'm still alive!"

I refused to allow myself to indulge in obsessions about pity or injustice although I could have made a case for both. Just like playing soccer, when your defense is weakened and the offense is running up the score you anticipate your next move in hopes of stopping them and turning the game around. I quickly recognized that I needed to act and act fast.

I reached out to several athletic directors at other institutions who I knew and respected to seek their advice. I received the same response from all of them. "She gave you no choice." They all agreed I had to fight back. You just don't dismiss a head coach two weeks into preseason unless he or she has done something major – sleeping with a student, embezzling funds or committing some other felony. Although I had not been accused of any such deplorable behavior, people would naturally assume that I was guilty of a major infraction or crime. I couldn't let that stand. I had no choice. I had to clear my name. I had no desire to become knotted up in litigation, but if I just walked away, everyone would assume that I did something wrong. To the contrary; my performance was off the charts. *She gave me no choice.*

My thoughts coalesced around this outrageous retaliation. My phone was ringing off the hook from the media. I needed some steady advice. I had a good friend who was both an attorney and a big fan of the Nevada soccer program. I thought of him immediately.

"Marc, I . . . lost my job," I began, evoking a flood of responses of disbelief from my attorney friend.

I explained that Groth retaliated against me for reporting violations within her administration. I had gone to my direct supervisor, Cindy Fox, and told her that Rich Merritt, the men's golf coach, was waging bets on college sports, including Nevada Wolf Pack football and basketball games, which was in direct violation of NCAA regulations and a serious threat to the athletic program.

There were also complaints against Merritt for hazing activities – including paying female student-athletes to eat the regurgitated food of other student-athletes, and giving cash, booze, and plane tickets to his athletes; all of which were violations of NCAA rules. Merritt also physically assaulted one of his male golfers, hitting him in the face. Obviously, he was bad news and needed to be gone. He was jeopardizing the welfare of the student-athletes and the integrity and reputation of the university. He was putting all of us, and the entire sports program at Nevada, at risk. I had no second thoughts about reporting him. Someone had to protect the powerless student-athletes. Someone had to protect the university. The report was contained within the athletic department and could be taken care of internally without bringing in an outside organization – namely, the NCAA – and without stirring up bad publicity that would accompany such exposure.

During my tenure, I had also stood up for my female athletes when I recognized that they were being discriminated against in violation of Title IX of the Federal Education Amendments of 1972. I nearly spit out my coffee when Nevada Associate Athletic Director Keith Hackett explained to me that my team would not be allowed to use our locker room for our Friday home games throughout the season because the VISITING football team would need to store its equipment in there for the football game the following day. The soccer team's locker room was also the visiting football team's locker room. I am a "team player" as noted by my supervisor in my personnel evaluations. I get it. I was willing to share. But don't tell me that the VISITING football team's *equipment* gets priority over *Nevada's own student-athletes!* No way, no how was I going to let that happen. I was a champion for my student-athletes. I fought for them. And since I went to battle for them, my student-athletes in turn played hard for me. I eventually convinced the administration that their plan was wrong on so many levels. The visiting football team would have to be inconvenienced. The Nevada soccer team would be using its locker room on game day. But that was not a battle that I should ever have had to fight.

> You always fought for us and I wanted to make sure you knew how much that meant not only to me, but the rest of the players as well. You were a round the clock coach and cared about us as individuals, and were always there on and off the field.
>
> – Nevada student-athlete

I also took issue when, without notice, my student-athletes were locked out of our locker room to accommodate youth football camps during our critical summer training period. The Nevada football team's locker room was 20 yards away, yet it was not being used for the football camp. The Nevada football players had full access to their locker room. My athletes, on the other hand, were locked out. I ran this issue up the proper channels to Cindy Fox, Keith Hackett, and the assistant football coaches. I explained to them that by addressing these concerns, I was protecting, not only my student-athletes, but the athletic department and its athletic director and, most importantly, the university. If a student or parent had brought Title IX charges against the school, the university would be vulnerable to substantial liability. I shared with Keith and Cindy that in 2000, female students at Louisiana State University sued their school for refusing to offer them athletic participation opportunities equal to those offered to male students. The court held that LSU discriminated against its female students in violation of Title IX. This was serious stuff and we were vulnerable.

"You have brought class, passion, and focus to this program."

– Lori Hadlock (Athlete's Parent)

In my world, when an individual accepts a head coaching position, he or she is accepting the responsibility to lead the young people of the program – to fight for them and protect them. Any leader worth his or her salt would have the same philosophy, and just as I had, would act accordingly when faced with knowledge that was potentially destructive.

After Marc got over the initial shock of what happened to his successful head coach friend, he gave me the advice that I sought.

"If you want your job back, you'll have to file a complaint for an administrative hearing as soon as possible," Marc told me. "You only have ten days so I'll get started on the paperwork first thing in the morning."

"Ten days?" I asked.

Marc explained that, under Nevada law, a retaliation complaint – that is, seeking reinstatement for a position lost in retaliation for reporting wrongdoing within a state entity – had to be filed within ten days of the perceived retaliation. Even with an immediate filing, however, the hearing would not be held for several months. I hoped against hope that it wouldn't lead to that, that cooler heads would prevail before the hearing.

I sat and stared at the phone after we hung up. Ten days? Only ten days to try to recover your entire career? All those years and effort and education and hopes for the future and you're allowed only ten days to try to salvage your life's work, your dreams? It didn't seem adequate. How many people know about that law? I hadn't. My guess . . . that's just the way the state of Nevada wanted it.

But thank God for Marc. I had to let go of those negative thoughts and consider myself fortunate to have someone who could look out for me. He'd file the necessary papers and I'd be well on my way back to getting my job. That's all I wanted. And, since Cary Groth had admitted in the presence of Gena Jones, the Assistant Vice President of Human Resources, that she had no grounds to end my employment, it would just be the formality of an official hearing – if that – and I'd be back where I belonged. In the meantime though, the team was struggling on the field, starting the season with three losses and no wins.

Marc filed the retaliation complaint on the tenth day and Nevada was officially on notice. But Marc had been right about the delay. The case would not be heard for five months.

It was an anxious time but as Marc and I could see it, it would be game over for the university once it went to a hearing because all the evidence was on our side, including Groth's direct admission of retaliation to me in the presence of Gena Jones. Marc and I knew Nevada would want to avoid a lawsuit and its associated damages, which would have to be filed separately from the administrative reinstatement hearing. They could not let this matter go to trial because a jury would immediately recognize that the evidence was overwhelmingly stacked against Groth and the university. I had no idea how right we were. I learned much later just how badly the university and its hired guns did not want this matter to go to trial, and to what lengths they'd go to in order to keep it out of the hands of a jury.

Marc and I laid out the time-line of the last seventy-four days of my employment at Nevada. On June 15th, I was given a merit raise based on my job performance over the past year. In the days following, I was presented with the initial proposed terms of a new multi-year contract. The contract extension would provide me with another pay increase and extend my employment for five years. And as a perk I would be provided with a new car fully paid for by the school. The expectation was that the contract would be finalized and presented to me for signature in August before the 2007-2008 season began.

While Groth and I were going back and forth sorting out the details of this new contract, women's golf coach, Jody Dansie, came to me quite upset. I had known Jody from my days at ASU. She had been a senior golf student-athlete when I was the young head coach of the ASU soccer program. I had also been on the committee that hired Jody as Nevada's women's golf coach. And after she came on board, we became close friends. But we were more than that. Cary and Cindy had asked me to be Jody's mentor and help her with the development of her career and program at Nevada. On that June day, Jody was seeking my help and advice.

While Jody had been on a recent maternity leave, Rich Merritt, the men's golf coach, took on the duties of coaching the women's golf team along with his regular responsibilities with the men's team. After Jody returned, she learned that he had caused serious problems within her program, including the commission of several violations of NCAA rules.

Jody also shared with me what both she and the student-athletes were aware of; that Merritt was heavily engaged in sports wagering, a major NCAA violation. But he wasn't just casually betting on random teams, he was also placing bets on Nevada football and basketball games. If the students or parents or anyone else for that matter reported any of this behavior directly to the NCAA – especially the sports betting – Nevada would be vulnerable to significant sanctions.

Dan Beebe, former NCAA Director of Enforcement, former NCAA Investigator, and former Commissioner of the Big 12 Conference and the Ohio Valley Conference, put it this way in an interview with the *Tulsa World* in December 2012:

> Gambling is such a serious violation in terms of the possible effect on the integrity of sports. With pro sports (and) college sports, all of us live in fear of whether or not somebody – an official, a player, a coach, an administrator was involved in gambling, and that's why there's such scrutiny about it (*Hoover*).

Dennis Dodd of CBS Sports described how crucial adherence to the NCAA's gambling regulations is:

> Gambling is the NCAA's capital murder charge. *Everyone* from Division III to the Final Four knows that. Keeping the slimy specter of gambling out of amateur athletics is the only thing that keeps NCAA sports legitimate (*Dodd*).

It was a huge problem. Jody had come to me because I was her friend and mentor. But now I had a moral obligation to go to Cindy with what Jody had told me. Under NCAA rules, all employees and student-athletes were required to sign an oath declaring that they reported all NCAA violations that they were aware of. A failure to report known violations is a violation itself. Jody was terrified of Rich Merritt's reaction as well as that of the administration. I wasn't good at brushing things under the rug or sticking my head in the sand. I was not going to sit back and watch this blow up in Nevada's face. Our administration deserved to know. They needed to know. The student-athletes were aware of Merritt's misconduct and it would only be a matter of time before it was out. Merritt was so reckless that he had openly discussed specific Nevada football and basketball games that he had placed bets on. He was even heard by one employee telling the Nevada basketball coaches: "Make sure you guys cover the spread tonight." I had worked at ASU during the period when it was recovering from a major NCAA sports betting scandal in its basketball program. That case led to federal indictments and prison time for those involved. The damage affected all of us. No sports were immune. We all had to deal with the negative fallout in our recruiting efforts. The reputation of ASU was tarnished. I did not want to go through that again. So on June 25th, I disclosed what I had learned to my direct supervisor, friend, and mentor, Cindy Fox, who then reported it to Groth and to Nevada's Director of Compliance, Sandie Niedergall.

On July 27th, the vice president of the university, Cindy Pollard, praised my service and community outreach activities on behalf of the university in an email to Cary Groth, which I was copied on. I had represented the university in an outreach initiative and my contributions were being recognized in the president's office.

On July 30th, Cindy Fox sent me an email regarding my contract negotiations. In it she wrote, "I want you to be here [at Nevada]."

August 7th was the day my student-athletes complained about being locked out of their locker room for football camp, resulting in my subsequent discussions with Keith Hackett and Cindy Fox about Nevada's vulnerability under Title IX. The report was passed along to Groth and I assumed that she would do the responsible thing and educate the assistant football coach on the importance of showing all of our athletes respect.

On August 13th, the conference coaches selected Nevada as the overwhelming favorite to win the conference in the pre-season soccer coaches poll.

On August 20th, Groth received the results of Nevada's internal investigation into the allegations of NCAA violations in the golf program. The report confirmed that Merritt had violated several NCAA rules while overseeing both the men's and women's golf programs. I would later learn that Merritt was a personal favorite of Groth's.

On August 22nd, I met with Groth to finalize the terms of the multi-year contract extension. I was stunned when I looked at the page that she slid across the table to me. The contract terms read 2.5 years, not the 5 years we had previously discussed. The courtesy car was removed from the offer sheet, and the financial terms were $10,000 less than I had previously discussed with her. The term sheet was dated August 21st, which meant that Groth had changed the terms of the offer the day after she received the report from the compliance office confirming the golf coach's NCAA violations. I'm not a pushover and I could see that Groth was trying to provoke me with a retaliatory offer. I didn't accept or reject the offer on the spot. I pointed out the differences between the extension previously discussed and the current one being offered to me. I left the meeting with contract in hand. I was told to get back to her with a decision.

So in response, on August 26th, I outlined my concerns to Groth that my contract had been diminished from what was first presented to me in retaliation for the subsequent NCAA and Title IX violations that I had brought to the university's attention. I respectfully requested that we table negotiations until after the season. I wanted to focus on my team. I was secure in my ability to lead them to another conference championship and NCAA tournament bid. We could meet again about a contract after the season.

On August 27th, Groth met with legal counsel, the university president, and Gena Jones of HR for the first time to seek approval to end my tenure.

I was notified the next day, August 28th, at the meeting with Groth. The exchange that was made in front of Gena Jones, bears repeating:

"Terri you're a great, great coach. Nobody can deny that. I just need to move on. I looked in your personnel file. There was nothing to use against you."

"This has whistleblower retaliation written all over it," I responded.

"I know," replied Groth.

On September 18th, a letter of reprimand from Cary Groth, Director of Athletics, and Jean L. Perry, Ph.D., Special Assistant to the President of UNR, was delivered to Rich Merritt, Head Men's Golf Coach, which provided him with the results of the internal investigation. It read, in part:

> The University of Nevada has determined that you have been involved in four NCAA bylaws violations. These violations are a result of your having paid for a meal for student-athletes in addition to providing the full per diem, your having paid cash to a student-athlete on two

different occasions as a result of a "dare," your having "swapped" a frequent flyer award ticket with a student-athlete who at the time did not have an award to "swap" and your having provided *false or misleading information concerning each of the preceding violations, the last violation is particularly disappointing.*

Emphasis added — I found it interesting to read that Groth was disappointed that Merritt had lied. She would live to be similarly disappointed in herself in the not-too-distant future. The letter concluded with a warning that if he provided false or misleading information or violated university policies in the future, he would be subject to termination.

Now mind you, I had a clean NCAA compliance record, and I had never been the recipient of a letter of reprimand during my entire tenure. My personnel file was spotless. And ironies of ironies, I was gone for REPORTING the NCAA infractions cited above which Merritt was found GUILTY of committing. Ultimately, Merritt's punishment for being in violation of four NCAA rules and for lying repeatedly to Nevada's compliance officer was a three-match suspension. He was not allowed to coach three fall golf competitions and he had to apologize to his team. I learned later that this was Merritt's second letter of admonishment for violating NCAA rules. The first letter had been issued to him less than a year earlier, for recruiting violations.

The sports betting and other NCAA violations aside, how many times did Rich Merritt have to hit a student-athlete — which was verified by both Merritt and the athlete — before he would be fired? Once should have been enough. The NCAA rulebook does not address such behaviors as physical assault or coercing an athlete to eat the vomit of another. The NCAA understandably expects university athletic directors and presidents to recognize that physical abuse of athletes by coaches does not meet its standards of ethical conduct — and beyond that it is criminal behavior. Groth had a chance to be a champion for the welfare of the student-athletes. But she failed. Instead she inexplicably chose to latch her career to her golf coach by protecting a coach that was not worth protecting.

Even before I had learned about the issues within the men's golf program, I was bothered by Merritt's behavior. My office was across the hall from the volatile golf coach and I soon became aware of his violent and unprofessional tendencies. The women's golf coach's office was next door to mine and we shared a common wall in the Athletic Department offices. On several occasions when Merritt had stopped by to meet with her, his angry outbursts knocked framed photos and certificates off the wall and onto the floor in my office. It was fortunate that I didn't have a new recruit or a parent in my office at those explosive moments. I had never witnessed such behavior in an office setting before. I couldn't help but wonder if Cindy, who was Merritt's supervisor as well as mine, was aware of his anger problem.

I looked back to my college experience and felt so fortunate to have played for a coach who had meant so much to me and my career. The comparison didn't put Merritt in a very good light. It was obvious to anyone who spent time around him and his program that his athletes were shortchanged on a special time in their young lives. Some of his athletes would later admit that they wanted to come forward and report his wrongdoing but were afraid to do so.

*   *   *

It was an anxious time between the filing of my papers and the date on which my reinstatement hearing was set. This whole concept of work place retaliation was something so far out of my realm. Retaliation to me was something that happened on the playing field. It was a bad response to a hard foul. Something the referees usually caught. The administrative hearing officer (AHO) would pull a red card on Groth's retaliation and I would soon be back at work.

But since the evidence was all on our side and the team was struggling on the field, Marc and I asked for a meeting with the university president prior to the hearing date. I wanted to get this whole mess behind me and get back to leading my team before their season was lost. Once the president realized the weight of evidence on my side, he would clean this up and reinstate me.

All I wanted was my job back.

So in hopes of settling the matter early, Marc and I arranged a meeting with Milton Glick, Nevada's president, in October 2007. Nettie had been named the interim head coach and the team was floundering. I wanted to get back to try and salvage the once-promising season. By this time, Glick had to be aware that Gena Jones of HR had witnessed Groth's admission that she had retaliated against me. Glick had no choice but to do right by me, by the university, and by the student-athletes . . . or so we thought. I was not asking for money, only my job back. I didn't know it at the time but later under oath Glick admitted that the university had received a large number of complaints about Groth's decision from parents, student-athletes and members of the community. Unknown to me, he was in possession of these letters of support for me prior to my meeting with him.

At our meeting, Glick was accompanied by Mary Dugan – the general counsel with the soccer-playing triplets. I asked them to handle this matter internally, which was the way it had started out and the way I intended it to be dealt with. They said little but feverishly wrote down every word I uttered. I told them it was a risk to support the golf coach who was putting the entire athletic program and university in a tentative position. It would be best for them to do a legitimate investigation of him rather than force the NCAA to do it. Glick was noticeably shaken by what I shared with him and said he needed a few days to review the matter. But he didn't need a few days as it turned out. A mere fifteen hours later, I was offered a settlement of two-month's salary, along with my agreement to turn over any evidence of wrong-doing I possessed to Glick and my promise to never set foot on campus again.

My recent presence at the soccer games as a fan in the stands was clearly not sitting well with the administration. I had no qualms about coming onto campus because I had done nothing wrong and had nothing to hide. But I was a constant reminder to them of their wrongdoing. And as the losses were adding up for the team, the pressure was mounting on Groth.

My reaction to the settlement offer was, "No way."

They didn't get it.

All I wanted was my job back.

CHAPTER 4

The Campus Culture

*"You will never do anything in this world without courage.
It is the greatest quality of the mind next to honor."*
~ *Aristotle*

I had no desire to file a claim against the university to recover financial damages. I did not want to be tied up in years of litigation. I simply wanted my job back, and I thought I could accomplish that through the administrative hearing process. However, after meeting with university president Milton Glick in October, I was incensed. He showed his cards and revealed his character in the insulting settlement offer fifteen hours post-meeting. This was a man not interested in doing right. He was only interested in making things go away. He made it clear that he was going to protect a morally bankrupt golf coach and an admitted retaliator in Athletic Director Groth . . . student-athletes be damned. Adding insult to injury, he wanted me to disappear from the campus after I had played by the rules and won a championship for the university. On the advice of Marc, I hired a new employment attorney named Jeff, who was experienced in litigation against the university. Jeff advised me to initiate a claim as soon as possible if I wanted to get the process moving and my life back. It was clear the administration was digging its heels in, and was not going to bring this to a quick good-faith resolution. I did everything in my power not to file a lawsuit. I did not want to go there but, due to the extraordinary circumstances involved, I felt that "I had no choice." On November 7, 2007, the day after the once-promising soccer season ended with a 6-11-1 record under Nettie's leadership, Jeff initiated proceedings in state court naming Cary Groth and the Nevada System of Higher Education (NSHE) as defendants.

On a parallel track, the administrative hearing to get my job back finally took place over four days in January and February of 2008, and included the depositions of several university administrators and employees. Jeff and I were very confident in the case we presented to the AHO. It was just a matter of time now and I would be reinstated as the head soccer coach at Nevada.

Or so I thought.

*   *   *

In the direct aftermath of my Nevada tenure, I had initially felt alone and abandoned. But I would soon learn that I didn't stand alone at all. There were others who were dealing with mistreatment and damage by forces within the university along with its many unofficial and powerful allies in the judicial system and media. It was also confirmed to me that illegal and unethical behavior was condoned and protected throughout the campus and was not isolated in the athletic department.

As my situation dragged on and my story was bandied about in the press, other individuals who had been victims of the university's retaliation began to surface and reach out to me. I thought my experience was unique but I was *way* off base. I was stunned to learn that there had been many others who had been wronged by the university administration. Although I knew that I had done nothing to deserve the treatment I received, I felt vindicated when I learned that others had similar stories to tell either through their own experiences or those of close colleagues. I did not for one moment relish anyone's problems with the university because I knew firsthand how personally and professionally devastating it was to go through such an ordeal. But I valued the support I received from these individuals who became friends of mine – friends who shared the bond of having had similar and devastating experiences with the university.

Professors Rich Schweickert and Hussein S. Hussein and University Police Sergeant Lane Grow came forward and shared their stories with me and I began to realize just how perverse the university administration – General Counsel Mary Dugan and her team of outside attorneys in particular – was. Through these university employees, I learned of many accounts of targeted abuse and unfair treatment that directly touched them and others who had suffered under the university's unscrupulous and unethical behavior. What they told me was shocking and would have been unbelievable if I hadn't already had an intimate knowledge of the dark side of Nevada's administration.

Dr. Hussein was an associate professor and researcher of animal nutrition at Nevada. He was a member of the faculty long before I was hired, joining the school in 1997. One of his responsibilities in his capacity in Nevada's animal biotechnology department was conducting research using lab animals. Ultimately Dr. Hussein became a whistleblower on department chair Esmail Zanjani.

When Dr. Zanjani joined the Nevada faculty in 2002, he had been an employee of a private company, Sierra Biomedical Research Corporation, which had been categorized as a non-profit organization under Nevada state statute. This corporation had been the recipient of federal funds through the National Institutes of Health, or NIH, to conduct medical research that required lab animal experimentation. After he was hired by Nevada, Dr. Zanjani maintained his association with Sierra Biomedical and continued to receive federal funds not for the university but for Sierra Biomedical – a clear violation of university rules and state laws. None of these federal funds – direct or indirect – were used for university projects or research. Further, Zanjani used his influence as department chair to hire two of his Sierra Biomedical researchers for faculty positions at the university. Zanjani and his employees then used the university's facilities and staff to conduct their Sierra Biomedical research under the federal funding.

Dr. Zanjani should have terminated his relationship with Sierra Biomedical when he accepted a faculty position at the university. Millions of dollars in federal funds were going to Sierra Biomedical research – but Zanjani was utilizing university staff and facilities paid for by taxpayers to subsidize research at his private business. Unbelievably, Zanjani was on the payroll at Nevada while at the same time he and Sierra Biomedical were profiting from federal funding for the research he was conducting on university property. Dr. Hussein also learned that Zanjani was ordering far more animals than was normally required for the research he was conducting and was profiting from them by reselling them at huge mark-ups to other researchers and universities around the country and even around the globe.

But there was another element to Dr. Hussein's allegations, in fact, a strange and almost sci-fi or horror-film twist. One of the research projects that Zanjani was conducting involved the injection of lab animals – specifically pregnant ewes – with human stem cells. The idea behind this work was that after human stem cells developed in the organs of the sheep and fetuses, livers and hearts could be harvested from them that would be suitable for human transplantation.

Federal law required that animals injected with human cells be incinerated to protect the environment from contamination because the animals could harbor viruses toxic to humans. Dr. Hussein learned that the animals were not being incinerated even though funding was provided for the cremation of the animals. This funding apparently landed in the profit pile for Sierra Biomedical and Zanjani. Instead of following protocol, the sheep were sent to a university-owned ranch to graze and reduce the invasive weeds on the property. After the animals had sufficiently done their clean-up work, they were left exposed to the elements and killed by predators or were shot and killed and buried on the ranch. Dr. Hussein and a local reporter uncovered hundreds of carcasses of ewes that had been injected with human stem cells. Dr. Hussein had photographic evidence of this horrific discovery. Another way Zanjani's employees illegally disposed of animal carcasses was by dumping them in open trenches near neighborhoods in Reno. Dr. Hussein also discovered other grisly cases of animal abuse on campus. Subsequently, Dr. Hussein reported this operation to the US Department of Agriculture (USDA) who, following a seven-month investigation, cited the UNR College of Agriculture with fifty-six violations of the Animal Welfare Act (AWA). The USDA offered the university the choice of settling the case and paying a fine or facing criminal charges. The university settled but got off easy because they were disingenuous and dishonest, refusing investigators full access to the lab animals. One of Dr. Hussein's graduate students accused university officials of trying to intimidate her in retaliation for her cooperation in the USDA probe.

Dr. Hussein had no animosity toward Zanjani; in fact, he had been on the committee that decided to hire him. Hussein felt it was the right and responsible thing to do to report Zanjani's illegal animal abuse for profit operation and the resultant animal abuse. But it wasn't Zanjani who wound up on the hot seat. Dr. Hussein was ultimately fired by Milton Glick, the university president, in April 2008, despite the fact that he had brought millions of dollars in grants to the university for his internationally recognized research expertise. Dr. Zanjani did not lose his job and remains employed by the university to this day.

Further support of Dr. Hussein's allegations came to light when a national research watchdog organization dubbed the University of Nevada, Reno the "worst lab in the nation" because it accumulated more federal animal welfare violations in less time than any other research institution in recorded history. Another complaint was filed with the USDA seeking federal fines against UNR in August 2012, by an animal rights group over the deaths of three sheep that died from thirst – despite the fact that all the water any animal would need surrounded them.

Professor Schweickert, a member of the Geological Sciences faculty at Nevada, learned indisputably that a scientist, Dr. Patricia Cashman, hired by the university had forged signatures of her faculty committee to obtain her PhD from the University of Southern California. The matter, including forensic evidence and statements from her committee, was brought to the university's attention. One member of Cashman's Dissertation Committee called it "the worst academic fraud issue I've had in my entire career." UNR conducted no investigation and the woman remains employed by the university to this day. Instead of the university investigating Dr. Schweickert's allegations, HE was investigated for discrimination. It was another case of retaliation. He was persecuted for reporting this woman who had presented false information to the university in order to secure employment.

Dr. Schweickert was also a witness of the sexual abuse of a female colleague by Dr. Robert Karlin, who was the chair of the Geological Sciences Department at the university. Dr. Schweickert and Dr. Mary Lahren, a Research Associate Professor and PhD. in Geological Sciences, were part of a group of university faculty members who were on an excursion to conduct field research. Dr. Schweickert was looking directly at Dr. Karlin when Karlin took a length of PVC pipe and suggestively stuck it between the legs of Dr. Lahren as she was carrying some equipment. Others also witnessed this sexual assault of Dr. Lahren. Of course, Dr. Lahren was outraged and humiliated. The incident and her previous concerns about Karlin's behavior were reported to university administration. Ann Dougherty, head of the university's Affirmative

Action office, investigated the complaint, stood up against university pressure, and found probable cause in Dr. Lahren's sexual harassment case against Karlin. Evidence of several previous sexual harassment complaints against Karlin had also been found. Three weeks after she reported her findings, Dougherty was fired. Karlin remains employed at the university, despite its claims of "Zero Tolerance" for sexual harassment. The school has subsequently received other formal complaints of sexual abuse and harassment against the professor, including those filed by graduate students on the campus, but has failed to take action.

In retaliation for Dr. Lahren reporting the incident to Affirmative Action and to provoke her into resigning, the administration blocked all sources of funding to her research and refused to remove Karlin as her supervisor. Karlin reduced the number of hours Dr. Lahren worked which caused her to lose all funding at the university. Dr. Lahren was essentially made to take an adverse settlement to leave the university. She was forced out of her field of study as a result of the incident at Nevada and Nevada's failure to properly handle the case and punish the predator professor who ruined her academic career. Because of his honest witness statements in Lahren's case, the university administration began a defamation campaign against Dr. Schweickert, and his dean blocked his access to research funds, ultimately destroying his research team.

Lane Grow was a university police officer who complained about mistreatment of fellow officers who spoke out against violations of university policies and state laws that were putting students at risk. He also complained when the Deputy Chief repeatedly sent pornographic emails of college aged women to Chief Adam Garcia and other officers through the university email system. The emails, which were sent over a period of several months, were also sent to several other people outside the university. The Deputy Chief was also reportedly given a two-day suspension for drinking alcohol in the UNRPD Station. He was later promoted to director. He remains employed at the university.

Sergeant Grow shared examples of many violations and improprieties committed by members of the University of Nevada, Reno Police Department (UNRPD). The Police Department under Chief Garcia was used by University of Nevada administration as a "private police force" to protect the administration and to threaten and harass students and employees who reported wrongdoing. There have been many indiscretions and abuses of power under Garcia's tenure:

an officer threatened to kill a fellow cop; another was arrested for DUI and speeding while driving his PATROL CAR; another cop completed his watch while he was under the influence of alcohol and armed with a deadly weapon. Chief Garcia was involved in a wide range of other public scandals including a complaint filed by People for the Ethical Treatment of Animals (PETA) that accused an officer of abusing one of the K-9 dogs. The head of the Nevada State Law Enforcement Officers Association (NSLEOA) accused Chief Garcia of ignoring complaints that the dog had been repeatedly abused. Grow also reported that he had witnessed Chief Garcia under the influence of alcohol while at work.

Officer Eric Hague of the university police was ordered to avoid making DUI arrests but refused to comply with an order that he viewed as ludicrous – not arresting anyone for drunk driving on a university setting seemed strangely counter-intuitive to him and a violation of his oath. He also refused to comply with another order not to cite or arrest university athletes or coaches – apparently no matter what they did. For his defiance, Hague was put on medical leave based on an EKG taken during a department physical that indicated he had a serious heart condition. He consulted with private doctors who gave him the all clear. He had no heart disease and the results of the department EKG were falsified apparently at the orders of . . . someone in power. On November 12, 2011, a local sports reporter was killed by a drunk driver on campus while crossing the street after a Nevada football game . . . just feet from the UNR police station.

In another widely reported story, Officer Kevin Youngflesh was arrested in 2004 on suspicion of drunken driving in an unmarked university police car after evading the arresting officer at high speeds. Despite this less than valorous performance, he was retained and later promoted. He was finally fired in 2008 after a fellow officer filed a complaint that Youngflesh had threatened to kill him in another alcohol-related incident. Word spread that Youngflesh was paid six figures by the university to "go away."

Another officer showed up for his shift on April 17, 2009, under the influence of alcohol. He was given a Preliminary Breath Test (PBT) by a fellow officer and, according to an internal university memo, blew a .17%, which was over twice the limit for a DUI in Nevada. The officer remained on his shift, working under the influence. All UNR police officers are required to carry a gun while on duty. He remained employed at the university for several more years.

Chief Garcia, on the other hand, had Officer Lane Grow arrested and fired for having Idaho license plates on his car. Lane had property in Idaho and owned multiple vehicles. Some were licensed in Nevada while others were legally licensed in Idaho. Out-of-state registration violations are normally treated with a warning, or at worst, a citation. However, Chief Garcia had Grow arrested, handcuffed, and booked in the county jail. Lane's "crime"? He had blown the whistle on police corruption within Garcia's department.

Chief Garcia withstood two letters of no confidence by his force. In February 2008, following a string of sexual assaults and the high-profile kidnapping and murder of a 19-year-old girl near campus, ten out of sixteen officers and all four sergeants sent a letter to the university president asking for Garcia to be fired. The letter claimed the force was undermanned and poorly equipped to deal with emergencies under Garcia's leadership.

In 2008, a consulting firm was hired to look at problems within the police department. The report concluded that the University of Nevada, Reno police department was "nearly crippled due to internal dysfunction" and had a "bunker mentality" among its ranks. Garcia has had over a dozen lawsuits filed against him. Yet he has weathered it all and he is still the Chief of Police.

The story now comes full circle back to Dr. Hussein. Homeland security camera systems were installed on university grounds on a $598,000 federal grant in 2003. As reported by Frank X. Mullen, Jr. of the *Reno-Gazette-Journal*, in an article entitled, "University of Nevada's Camera Network Raises Fear," Professor Hussein discovered a hidden homeland security camera had illegally been set up to monitor his activities and visitors at his lab offices. Dr. Hussein had previously found a hidden university police camera installed inside a smoke detector that was being used to monitor him.

It is noteworthy that this surveillance was set up after Hussein had disclosed the activities of Dr. Zanjani and had reported the animal abuse taking place at the university. Because of Dr. Hussein's reports he became a target of the university administration. Chief Garcia initially denied any involvement in the spy camera debacle but was later forced to admit that his department was behind nearly two years of video surveillance of Hussein.

Adam Garcia, campus police chief, at first said that his force had nothing to do with the homeland security video system. But UNR officials now admit that Garcia has full control of the camera (*Mullen*).

Chief Garcia was also involved in trumped up terrorist charges levied against Dr. Hussein, who is a native of Egypt. The FBI was called in to investigate Dr. Hussein and his lab. But he was immediately cleared.

The University of Nevada, Reno's culture of retaliation was also demonstrated in the case of Charles Stricker. Charles was an employee who sued his supervisor at the University of Nevada, Reno, locksmith department, for discrimination and retaliation. He claimed that he was retaliated against after complaining about pornography being displayed on computers in the workplace. Throughout this case the university's defendants, witnesses, and lawyers all testified falsely claiming that there was no pornography, rather the images were just photos of model Cindy Crawford. In his closing argument, the plaintiff's attorney displayed the photos that Stricker had complained about to the jury. There was no doubt in anyone's mind that the photos were clearly pornographic images of a woman who was not Cindy Crawford, proving that the university's case was built on lies, and that the witnesses had committed perjury.

The jury awarded Stricker twice what he asked for and, in an unusual move, the jury asked the judge to read a statement, signed by all jurors. The jurors delivered a message to the UNR administration:

We are appalled and deeply disappointed that through actions or inactions of management, administration and the university that this matter has come this far. It shows gross disregard for university policy, taxpayer's money, and the court's time and First Amendment rights.

But the UNR administration had its own unique take on this "message." Instead of heeding the reprimand by the jury and vowing to clean up their act, the lesson learned by university administration was that when the evidence was stacked against them, it was unwise to allow a complaint go to trial. But how could they control that?

I was being naïve and found that there were any number of ways to sabotage a case. All it took was the right people in the right places who had strings to pull and the willingness to pull them.

Gregory MacRenaris was the owner and operator of a private solar screen company. He discovered when his company was bidding for projects at the university that Buzz Nelson the Associate Vice President of the Facilities Services Department was awarding preferential contracts to Gardner Engineering. The preferential treatment of an individual or company on projects taking place on state property is unlawful in the state of Nevada. There was apparently a close relationship between Nelson and Jim Gardner, owner of Gardner Engineering. Frustrated that his company was never awarded a university project, MacRenaris obtained documents through the Freedom of Information Act that clearly showed Nelson's preferential treatment toward Gardner Engineering. In the minutes of a meeting with Gardner, an architect under Nelson stated in reference to a Gardner bid that "By doing things this way at least it looks like a legitimate bid." He went on to say, "Maybe other contractors will recognize this for what it is and not bid it." Evidence was uncovered that Gardner routinely padded their charges by ten percent on these illegal no-bid contracts. In the FOIA documents, MacRenaris also found evidence of improper use of emergency purchase orders, fictional maintenance problems, and cost splitting to avoid State oversight on bidding practices. The documents also proved that Gardner was being awarded the lion's share of university projects. MacRenaris also uncovered the questionable transfer of money from one department to another making it impossible to trace where the funds wound up. MacRenaris filed a civil suit about these violations but ultimately his case was set aside by the Nevada state Attorney General who told MacRenaris that "We're not dealing with this anymore." It was "game over" even though MacRenaris had proof to support his charges.

Hearing the details of the MacRenaris case was my first inkling that the university's reach went far beyond the perimeter of the campus.

The severity of the culture of retaliation on campus was further documented in the University of Nevada, Reno Faculty Morale Study

Report, dated August 2005, approximately one year after Mary Dugan was named General Counsel:

> A large number of respondents cited a climate of intimidation, fear and powerlessness among university faculty and staff. Some described their work environment as hostile and expressed concern for a lack of the rule of law on campus. It is noteworthy that within an academic community that espouses the principles of academic freedom, so many respondents took extraordinary measures to preserve their anonymity, expressing fear of retaliation or even termination for expressing their viewpoints *(Stitt)*.

There would be eventual fallout from my case as well. Human Resources representative Gena Jones and Director of Compliance Sandie Niedergall both left the university shortly after giving their depositions. Gena was present at my final meeting with Groth and corroborated my claim that Groth admitted she was retaliating against me for reporting violations. Sandie was responsible for conducting the university's investigation of Rich Merritt and the golf program. She gave damaging testimony against the university and her supervisor, Dr. Jean Perry. Sandie had been employed by Nevada for 15 years before she packed up and moved east.

The retaliation on the Nevada, Reno campus resulted in a wave of lawsuits filed against the university. In July 2008, the *Reno Gazette Journal* published an article, "UNR Outside Legal Fees Hit $1.7 million." At this time in 2008, UNR had forty cases pending against it. The university had spent over $1.7 million hiring outside law firms to help defend against just four of those cases. It could provide no estimates of how much had been spent by its in-house lawyers in defense of these lawsuits. These costs were about to go up, way up in defending my case alone.

The University of Nevada is not the educational safe haven that the average student, parent, professor and administrator would naturally expect. It is a den of crime and money laundering in an establishment where no one would suspect such activities would take place. The university police do protect and serve but only the university's administration and General Counsel. The tactics of Nevada's leadership and its police force included spying, manufacturing evidence, allowing "select" individuals to go unpunished for wrongdoing, and harassing, threatening and framing those who dared to look out for the integrity and reputation of an institution of higher learning – an institution that made up its own rules and laws as required to maintain its power and the status quo.

The administration used taxpayer money and federal funds to protect people who have committed animal abuse, sexual harassment, fraud, embezzlement, perjury, retaliation, and violations of the public trust. That is a provocative statement to be sure.

But I lived through the ravages of this corruption.

So, please read on, I'll prove every word of it.

CHAPTER 5

A Game of Cat and Mouse

"That which does not kill us makes us stronger."
~ Friedrich Nietzsche

Although my reinstatement hearing was just the tip of the iceberg of what simply began as a rightful attempt to get my job back, it morphed into a seemingly endless game of cat and mouse. In the scheme of things, one could say that the administrative hearing that took place under the authority of the State of Nevada's Department of Personnel was just a minor blip down a road that was littered with far greater legal challenges. But putting the spotlight on this rather mundane process serves to illustrate the incompetent, dishonest and deceptive nature of a state system that sets the grueling course for a state employee who suffered retaliation.

And despite trying for years to have a just resolution in my case, the Department of Personnel – DOP – wasn't equipped to provide that. I realized much later that I never had a chance from square one to get an honest decision from that Department. The DOP was charged by state statute to give me a fair hearing. Instead it sided with the university that submitted evidence that was proven to be fraudulent right there at the hearing. Perhaps the department was serving two Gods – the State of Nevada and those hidden behind the State Flag who actually ran things. Ironically, it seemed the Department of Personnel was least concerned with the "personnel."

The delays and procedural red tape involved in it was a true test of my patience – a test that I wasn't passing. Bottom line, while it dragged on it wasn't doing what I wanted it to do for me; simply put, to get my job back. And beyond that, it wasn't functioning as it should. I had the right to a swift disposition of my complaint. I had the evidence on my side and should have been reinstated in my coaching position at Nevada. I should have been given a clear-cut thumbs up or thumbs down strictly based on factual evidence as presented at the hearing. But I didn't get that. If the DOP had done its job it would have been case closed and the taxpayers of the state wouldn't have been forced to support four years of administrative hearings about the same case – a case that could have easily and equitably been resolved in a matter of days.

The first decision coming out of the Nevada Department of Personnel about my complaint was not in my favor. I knew that the preponderance of evidence – no check that . . . that all of the evidence – was on my side, that the decision was wrong and that I was being railroaded.

Although Nevada was an "*employment-at-will*" state, meaning that an employer could terminate an employee at any time and without any reason, my situation did not fall under that statute. Since I was a state employee who had reported wrongdoing within a state-operated organization the university had to show cause for ending my employment, and it had to demonstrate that its decision was not based on retaliatory reasons. Groth had admitted that there was no "cause" and that she acted in retaliation for reporting violations within her department. Because of this, what the administrative hearing officer (AHO), under someone's direction, was forced to do was to accept the lies, false testimony and manufactured evidence to support the "cause" that he was charged with finding. But because the university legal team had virtually nothing to work with in presenting their case, the AHO went above and beyond, curing their deficiencies and manufacturing findings on the university's behalf. The AHO was hired and paid by the State. The same State that was liable for damages if an employee received a favorable decision against a state entity, in this case the university. The conflict of interest was obvious.

As soon as the decision against me was announced, Jeff immediately filed an appeal and proved in court that the administrative hearing had been rigged. It was remanded back to the Nevada Department of Personnel where it was thrown out again, this time on a technicality. But we weren't done yet. After another appeal, it was once again remanded back to the DOP for a hearing on the fraudulent conduct that engulfed my initial hearing. I felt I was watching a tennis match from the perspective of the ball.

Although my original complaint had been submitted in a timely manner, ten days after Groth's retaliation in September 2007, in 2010, the hearing was still bouncing around the Nevada State Personnel Department. I only had ten days to file the necessary papers to have a chance at saving my job. As it turned out, the state had four years to try to wrest it from me permanently.

The original AHO was suspended from duty based on his actions and demonstrated incompetency in my case. That little bit of justice felt good but of course it wasn't nearly enough. The lop-sided system for reinstatement through the DOP was a joke. What was ironic was that when I initially filed and learned that my administrative hearing would take several months to be heard, I thought that was too long. Little did I know how slow the wheels of justice turned and how they sometimes didn't really turn at all, and sometimes they even got stuck in reverse.

Since the never ending personnel hearing is undoubtedly confusing to anyone who hadn't lived it, I believe that a description of the events and meetings would not only be appropriate but helpful in order to understand the ridiculous process that I had to endure.

The hearing was scheduled for January and February 2008. I was on time with my filing but . . . there apparently was no defined deadline for the State of Nevada to resolve my complaint because they were, well, they were the State of Nevada. The hearing was a four-day session during which the AHO heard evidence and took depositions. Everything went as I expected because I was telling the truth about what happened and had witnesses to verify my statements. The AHO took it under advisement and declared that he would announce his decision after his review – which we knew, by then, wouldn't happen at lightning speed.

In March 2008, the decision was finally rendered on my administrative hearing. The AHO said that I did not meet my burden of proving retaliation.

He said I hadn't met my burden of proof? But I had. With Groth's statement that she "looked in my personnel file and had nothing to use against me," and that she knew that my case had "whistleblower retaliation written all over it," it was indisputable proof. Maybe it wasn't a wise admission on her part but it was unambiguous. In the five years that it took my case to come to final resolution, that incriminating, damning statement was never denied by Groth. And her admission was witnessed by Gena Jones, the Human Resources Assistant VP, and later attested to by Jones in her deposition. It was that simple and it was that crystal clear. Based on this one factor alone, it should have been a win for me. Yet, the official finding was that I had not proven that I was retaliated against even though the person who ended my tenure admitted it.

I was stunned. This was my first taste of the Nevada Injustice System, but it wouldn't be my last.

The AHO ignored blatant perjury that was exposed in his presence at the hearing along with fabricated evidence, including a falsified personnel evaluation that UNR had tried to submit. HR had submitted my entire personnel file previously to the AHO and he had my authentic evaluations. I didn't initially know the full scope of the lies and deception that was part of that first hearing. The truth trickled out over the years as my case roared along at a snail's pace.

University attorney, Assistant General Counsel Charles Hilsabeck, admitted that the personnel evaluation he was trying to submit was not genuine after we exposed it in front of the AHO. I had received "commendable" personnel evaluations all three years. The university admitted that I was one of only four head coaches to receive "commendable" evaluations all three years during my tenure. In other words, by their own admission, I was one of their top four performing coaches out of a total of sixteen head coaches. Hilsabeck had tried to replace my 2005 "commendable" evaluation with a "satisfactory" evaluation. The fabricated personnel evaluation was signed by Cindy Fox, which hurt. Jeff called out UNR in front of the AHO forcing a red-faced Hilsabeck to sheepishly withdraw the false evaluation from the evidence. Did the AHO somehow miss that exchange?! Or perhaps he was clouded by his own admission that he was a fan of the Nevada Wolf Pack.

The process allowed for the opportunity to appeal an AHO's decision in the district court. We filed a notice of appeal on March 10, 2008, within days of the final decision. The case was so wrought with fraud that Jeff decided that we needed to take a safe and circuitous route around the system and not go down the standard appeal route. Rather than file a standard opening brief, we filed two separate and distinct emergency motions for remand due to the fraudulent conduct by UNR and the AHO. A motion is a request directly to the judge. We were asking the judge to remand the case back to the DOP for consideration of newly discovered evidence that was concealed by the university and which exposed their fraudulent conduct at the hearing. This was not the trial of the century – in fact it wasn't even a trial. It was a simple personnel hearing. But as my case unfolded over the years, there was never anything simple about it.

On March 10, 2009, we won our emergency motions for remand and the district court judge sent the case back to the AHO to consider the fraudulent conduct of Cary Groth and the university lawyers Mary Dugan and Charles Hilsabeck. Consideration of the fraud committed by the AHO was also a part of the remand order.

The *Reno Gazette Journal* – the only newspaper in town – refused to report that my case had been remanded (re-opened and sent back for further review) despite their knowledge of this fact. I learned along the way that the RGJ – under the leadership of Executive Editor Beryl Love – was reluctant to print anything damaging about the university. I would discover later that there was a close relationship between the RGJ leadership, university administrators, and the private attorneys on UNR's payroll – truly small town stuff for the "biggest little city in the world."

In late March 2008, just days after the first AHO – Bill Kockenmeister – had rendered the astonishing decision in my case, I had read that his contract was up for renewal. After speaking with Jeff, UNR Police Sergeant Lane Grow and I appeared at the public comment session of the open meeting for the Nevada Department of Personnel. Lane had witnessed Kockenmeister oversee another UNR case involving a police officer and reported that Kockenmeister had violated several laws and procedures to deliver a favorable decision to the UNR police chief – the same upstanding police chief whose force had rebelled against him for his lack of leadership and questionable and illicit activities.

After Lane and I addressed the Personnel Commission regarding Kockenmeister's nefarious conduct in my case and the case involving the police chief, Kockenmeister was suspended from receiving new cases for three months.

So on remand, I received a new AHO, Jay Short. Short's wife worked at the university. Short knew the rules of the game and was acutely aware that if he ruled in my favor his wife would be subject to termination. So, one week before my scheduled hearing in June 2010, rather than grant me a hearing to review the perjury and the fabricated and concealed evidence, he tossed out my case on a 'made up' technicality. He retired as an AHO one month later. Yet another year had passed before I had been able to get my case in front of this second AHO – Short – who unceremoniously dismissed it.

I had always believed that Jay Short intentionally made it easy for me to have his decision overturned. I am certain that he wanted no part of my high profile case and knew that he would not be the AHO on a second remand due to his impending retirement. He just wanted out. Short's behavior demonstrated that even these quasi-judicial officers understood and feared the reach of the university's retaliatory administration. So I appealed again to the district court and on December 14, 2010, I won a second remand, easily overturning Short's decision.

On remand I was assigned a new AHO because of Short's retirement. His name was Lansford Levitt. I learned that not only was his wife employed by UNR, but that he lied on his application for the AHO position. After Levitt was assigned to my case, I unexpectedly received some information in the mail from an employee of the DOP. The documents I received were Levitt's cover letter and resume that he had submitted when applying for the AHO position. I never requested this information and I was stunned that I had received it. Then it hit me that someone on the inside did not like the way his or her department was doing business, and was tipping me off. In his cover letter to the Personnel Commission, Levitt wrote that he had no conflict of interest with NSHE/UNR so he could oversee all cases that were filed with the DOP. It did not take much research to learn that his wife was a long-time employee of the university. Immediately after Levitt found out that I discovered this information, he deleted his wife's identity from his public Facebook profile. So, I had again been assigned an AHO who had the university paying his bills and putting food on his table. To make matters worse, he lied about his conflicts of interest on his application for employment. He obviously was not equipped with the requisite set of values necessary to pass judgment on a personnel or any other matter.

Prior to learning this information, we had a prehearing conference with Levitt. It was at this conference that I laid out all of the fraud, including perjury and fabricated evidence submitted by Athletic

Director Cary Groth, Executive Associate Athletic Director Cindy Fox, and UNR attorneys Dugan and Hilsabeck. Levitt shifted uncomfortably in his chair, as I meticulously laid out my case document by document, exposing one dreadful lie at a time. He was petrified of this case, of my evidence, and of the excruciating detail presented. UNR's expanding defense team squirmed in silence as several witnesses looked on.

But that would not stop Mary Dugan. I learned that a few days after this prehearing conference, UNR's new assistant general counsel Joe Ward paid a visit to Levitt in his Reno office to discuss my case. This was a meeting that Levitt not only participated in, but attempted to conceal from me. General Counsel Dugan knew she could not win on the merits so she dispatched her new assistant to intimidate the AHO. I learned this because I was inadvertently copied on an email that I was not meant to see. I'm making the case that my opponents were deceptive. I am not arguing that they were good at it. The fact that Dugan took such a risk proves that the university had no case.

Additionally, Levitt had also run into a mutual acquaintance of mine at the grocery store while my case was pending before him. The acquaintance called me and advised me to get Levitt off my case immediately. He was talking about my case in a very biased fashion. After disclosing Levitt's conduct to the Personnel Commission he was forced to recuse himself from my case. Unwilling to own up to his bad behavior, Levitt, a 60-something year old man, lashed out at me and called it a voluntary recusal in a disingenuous attempt to save face.

To recap, the case went through three AHO's up to this point, two who had spouses employed by the university along with one, an admitted fan of the Nevada Wolf Pack, who was suspended for incompetence. The incestuous culture of small town Reno seemed impossible to escape.

Adding further embarrassment to the DOP, the administrative assistant to the AHO, Joan Dinning, was let go immediately after she too engaged in questionable behavior. I received a personal apology from the Director, Teresa Thienhaus, after I was, once again, copied on an email that was not intended for me to see.

In September 2011, with a new administrative assistant in place at the DOP, the fourth AHO was assigned to this merry-go-round. Norman Hirata was from Las Vegas and worked at David C. Amesbury's law firm. Amesbury was indicted by the Feds in 2011 for his involvement in a massive corruption scandal involving police, lawyers, and judges in Vegas.

The case is still ongoing today and Justice Department lawyers from Washington D.C. are spearheading the investigation. Amesbury's wife, a Chief Deputy District Attorney in Las Vegas, has also been implicated. While my case was pending before Hirata, Amesbury was found lying in the street, "beaten to a pulp" in a gated upscale neighborhood late at night. Both of his kneecaps were shattered. This happened in October 2011, days after Amesbury agreed to a plea deal with the Feds in exchange for his testimony against others. Shortly thereafter, in March 2012, he was found dead in an apparent suicide. His death occurred just five days after another attorney implicated in the scandal was found dead. Two other people who attracted the interest of authorities in this sweeping investigation also died under unusual circumstances. This true story is straight out of Nevada folklore. Needless to say, I was not very confident that Hirata was on the up and up. The very public Amesbury scandal was going on while Hirata was assigned to my case.

I finally had a hearing scheduled before Hirata on June 19, 2012, to get my job back. This scam had gone on for four years. But days before the hearing, I withdrew the complaint. By this time I no longer wanted my job back. I was not going back to live in that state. I now recognized that I could never recruit a student-athlete to that university after what I had learned about the administration. It was not a safe place for anyone, employees or students. I was also aware by now that had I won reinstatement to my position, the university would have just appealed it and placed me on administrative leave. Around and around we would still be going. The liability was too great for UNR. My case was too high profile. And it was clear that through their arrogance and defiance of the law that they were never going to honor an order of reinstatement if one was issued. They had announced to my student-athletes even before my first hearing in 2008 that I was not getting my job back. They hired the replacement coach two weeks before my first hearing ever occurred and moved his family to Nevada from Texas. The university knew the administrative hearings were rigged; that the deck was stacked in the house's favor.

In December 2012, a newly hired AHO reinstated a UNR police officer to his position. In his order, the AHO found that university officials tampered with witnesses, committed perjury, and initiated an investigation of the police officer that "was not credible." The AHO found that the university's investigation was "unfairly skewed and result oriented"; it was conducted to support a predetermined result, the termination of this police officer. This new AHO, who displayed such courage in standing up to the system, was fired by the DOP three months later. He clearly had not gotten the memo that he was supposed to make calls for the home team. The university placed the police officer on leave – refusing to reinstate him – and appealed to the district court. The case is ongoing.

AHO Bill Kockenmeister, who was suspended for three months in the wake of my case, was later implicated in a bribery scandal in another case. His attempted bribe was in writing and turned over to the Personnel Commission by a former state employee, the recipient of the bribe. Kockenmeister remains employed by the DOP. AHO Lansford Levitt has been retained by the Commission despite his lie to the DOP on his application and his other misconduct in my case. The Personnel Commission continues to employ Kockenmeister and Levitt because they play by house rules.

The hearing was a ruse and a fraud. I realized I was in a kangaroo court – a sham of a legal proceeding where the decision is predetermined – that was offered by the state of Nevada to give the appearance of a fair legal proceeding. I had believed in the system but I never had a chance.

The university wasn't what it was portrayed to be on the glossy recruitment flyers sent to prospective students and their parents. It wasn't an oasis in the den of inequity otherwise known as the state of Nevada, it was part of it. The university was run by an unsavory administration that made up the house rules, but didn't play by them.

I no longer wanted my job back at Nevada.

CHAPTER 6

Embezzlement

"To those who cling to power through corruption and deceit and the silencing of dissent, know that you are on the wrong side of history."

~ President Barack Obama
Inaugural Speech, January 20, 2009

When General Counsel Mary Dugan and her team of in-house lawyers were not up to the task – which was often the case – Dugan would farm out legal work to politically connected private law firms with the tacit agreement of the Nevada Attorney General. McDonald Carano Wilson LLP – known simply as MCW – is a firm in Reno that was hired by Dugan to assist in Dr. Hussein's litigation. Kent Robison is an attorney for Robison Belaustegui Sharp & Low who was hired to assist in both Dr. Hussein's and my cases. The Attorney General paid the private law firms out of the general fund which apparently had unlimited public money. According to billing records, these private attorneys were paid in the millions of dollars for their work on UNR cases over several years. Apparently, there were no checks and balances when it came to the use of taxpayer funds by the AG's office.

The Nevada System of Higher Education enlisted these outside lawyers despite having its own stable of attorneys on staff. The staff attorneys were paid as system employees, three of whom had primary responsibility in my case – General Counsel Mary Dugan and Assistant General Counsels Joe Ward and Charles Hilsabeck. Cindy and Cary apparently did not trust the university lawyers and secured their own private attorneys to manage their involvement. John Arrascada represented Cary Groth, while Leif Reid, son of US Senator Harry Reid, looked out for Cindy Fox's interests.

General Counsel Dugan's husband, Dan Dugan – the man who tried to secure favors from the university for his local soccer club – has his own trial consulting business. He has been hired by both NSHE and Kent Robison to assist in litigation. So following the money, which history has taught us to do, the retaliation coordinated by General Counsel Dugan and her staff resulted in multiple lawsuits being brought against the university. In over her head, Dugan needed rescuing and felt compelled to hire Robison and pay for his services with taxpayer funds allocated from the AG's Office. Over the years, NSHE and Robison had hired Dan Dugan to consult on cases. Taxpayer money paid to Mary Dugan's husband landed back in the Dugan household and, in essence, went right into Mary Dugan's pocket. Mary Dugan used taxpayer dollars to subsidize the legal protection of UNR retaliation and, she in turn, profited from it.

*   *   *

After Dugan and her assistants used millions of dollars from the AG's general fund for legal defenses, Dugan was told to look for alternative sources to pay for the growing expenses originating from her office. Evidence secured by Dr. Hussein showed that Mary Dugan had been using state and federal funds from the UNR College of Agriculture to pay MCW. Large sums of money had been spent by the university – $60,000 to $100,000 per month – to cover legal expenses. The evidence included letters and invoices that revealed that Dugan's office was directing that the payment of a monthly invoice from MCW be split evenly between the College of Agriculture and the Office of Administration and Finance. But no state or federal appropriations existed that allow UNR to spend funds designated for the College of Agriculture for these types of expenditures. The money given to the university by the state and federal government for the College of Agriculture is allocated for teaching and research, not legal fees. Yet, the illicit attachment of these funds was an ongoing practice.

Evidence also indicated that the University of Nevada, Reno was double-dipping from the state and federal governments. The State of Nevada pays all the facilities and administrative costs – F&A costs – that are required in order to conduct research at the UNR campus. But the administration was also requesting and receiving F&A costs from the federal government for these same expenditures – knowing full-well that these costs had already been paid for by the State of Nevada. This surplus appeared to be a source for payment of some of the steep legal fees generated under Dugan's failed stewardship of the university's legal department.

* * *

Kent Robison's billing records revealed that he was charging the State for work that was well outside the scope of his contract. Prior to receiving a contract to assist on my case in 2009, Robison was contracted by the State for work only on Dr. Hussein's case against Defendant Mary Dugan. The contract's scope was strictly limited to that specific case – *Hussein v. Dugan*. However, Robison's billing records showed that he improperly billed the State for work that was done *before* the contract was issued, approved, or signed by the State Board of Examiners. He also submitted a long list of charges for work performed in defending other cases against UNR, falsely billing the State under the *Hussein v. Dugan* contract. The taxpayers also paid Robison $1,105 to meet with the *Reno Gazette-Journal* editors and reporters in an effort to improve the image of the University of Nevada, Reno, an image that was increasingly becoming a PR problem. Again, this was far outside the scope of his contract. Robison also billed $1,235 for communications with the UNR General Counsel's Office about a report they had received from the US Attorney's Office – a report leaked by the US Attorney detailing criminal activity on the UNR campus. More on this later. Robison's fraudulent billing practices reached my case as well. In January 2008, over one year before he was contracted by the State to work on my case, Robison billed the taxpayers $780 to falsify an affidavit for Mary Dugan.

In preparation for my reinstatement hearing, Groth had submitted an affidavit under the penalty of perjury that was contradicted by an official letter that Dugan had sent to my attorney Marc months earlier. After Groth lied under oath in her affidavit, we submitted Dugan's letter into evidence to prove that Groth had committed perjury. Dugan refused to testify at the hearing and instead submitted an affidavit. Knowing Groth was going to be exposed for committing perjury, Dugan put Robison to work. His January 23, 2008, billing record stated:

> Telephone conference with Mary Dugan regarding affidavit consistency with Groth affidavit and response to [Marc] Picker letter in Patraw case.

Forty-eight hours later Dugan submitted an affidavit attempting to alter her earlier statements in the letter to Marc. Robison and Dugan manufactured a new story in a poor attempt to achieve consistency with Groth's affidavit. But their efforts were for naught when Assistant Vice President of Human Resources Gena Jones testified and confirmed the accuracy of Dugan's initial letter to Marc exposing the perjury by Groth who, not surprisingly, faced no charges for her crime.

Robison's billing records proved to be a rich source of damning evidence against both UNR and Robison himself.

*   *   *

One day Dr. Rich Schweickert and I discussed a document that my attorney had received and that had struck me as rather odd. It was a billing record and donation of legal services from Cary Groth's personal attorney John Arrascada to the Athletic Association of the University of Nevada – AAUN. It stated that the staff member responsible for obtaining the services was Rory Hickok, the Associate AD who oversaw the AAUN. The AAUN is the central fundraising arm of Nevada athletics, a foundation that "provides the athletic department with private financial support for scholarships, facilities and operations." The AAUN was not a party to my case and had no liability whatsoever. They did not need legal representation, and Arrascada's statement made clear his donation was on behalf of Groth. The conclusion that was staring Rich and I in the face was disturbing. Was Groth embezzling money out of the AAUN to pay for her personal attorney's fees? The AAUN solicits money from Wolf Pack supporters to support the athletic programs and student-athletes, not to pay for the personal expenses of the athletic director. If Groth was paying legal fees out of the AAUN or any university account, it would be no different than her outright stealing money for groceries . . . or to support a gambling habit . . . from these accounts.

So Rich requested from the university all the billing records of private attorneys John Arrascada and Leif Reid that had been submitted to the AAUN and the university. Rich figured that if Groth was using university money to pay her private attorney, Cindy Fox might be too. It was a bit of a fishing expedition, but Rich caught the one that almost got away. While Dugan, who handled the public records requests for the university, stonewalled on Arrascada's records, she did produce Leif Reid's. Reid had submitted billing records to the university on behalf of Cindy Fox as late as October 5, 2010. Mark and Cindy Fox had resigned their positions at Nevada in 2009, and had moved to Georgia, a fact clearly known to Cindy's attorney. But Reid did not send the bill to Cindy Fox; he sent it to the Nevada athletic department. Because Arrascada had made clear that Associate AD Rory Hickok was the staff member responsible for his invoices, and Rory's financial responsibility was the oversight of the AAUN, Rich contacted Rory to request a review of the AAUN's books. The AAUN's books are public records and Nevada laws require that public records be made available for inspection upon request. Rory refused to respond to Rich. Undeterred, Rich showed up at Rory's office on multiple occasions only to be told each time that Rory was unavailable. If the books would show that no payment was made to Reid or Arrascada, why wouldn't Rory spend twenty minutes with Rich to prove it? Simply put, there is no plausible explanation as to why Cary Groth's and Cindy Fox's personal legal bills were sent to Rory Hickok and Nevada athletics. And, for this reason, both Rory and Mary Dugan refused to provide the records Rich requested.

Dugan and Rory went to great lengths to cover their tracks, sending Rich on a wild goose chase. After numerous communications between Dugan and Rich – because Rory refused to respond – Dugan produced only sanitized accounting statements of the AAUN that contained no specific individual invoices, payment statements, or names of vendors. These were not the billing records of the AAUN in the custody of Associate AD Rory Hickok. The open records law requires that the custodian of records – in this case, Rory – open his books to inspection to any member of the public upon request. But Rory refused to and instead hid behind Dugan.

General Counsel Mary Dugan and her staff of in-house and private attorneys were committing financial crimes to cover up other crimes committed on campus and in the courts. As the evidence will show, these lawyers' schemes were not limited to shady billing practices. With taxpayer money, these lawyers were paid to threaten and intimidate witnesses, falsify evidence, and defame the innocent. They were hired guns who, thanks to the good people of Nevada, were well-compensated and would stop at nothing to destroy those who dared to stand up to the rampant retaliation that existed on the university campus.

CHAPTER 7

Public Property

"You saw his weakness, and he will never forgive you."
~ Johann Schiller

I've learned a lot over the years since leaving Nevada. One of my biggest lessons was that only true friendships weather the worst storms. I have also learned to trust my better instincts. When Nettie's behavior had led me to question her loyalty to me and the program in my third season, I should have let her go right then and there. Unfortunately, the internal warning signs that I felt about her then were later confirmed repeatedly as my efforts to seek justice began to face increasingly strong headwinds.

Since I had an incredibly strong case and was showing no signs of dropping it, UNR administration officials were in full panic mode. They could not allow the volume of evidence I had against them to surface in open court. They were backed in the corner with only one option – they would have to pull out all stops to ensure that my case never went to trial. Their efforts to harass me and others involved a full range of approaches. When one didn't work, they tried the next. They tried to beat me down and, I must admit, that at times quitting seemed the only answer. But I couldn't. The damage they had caused me was too great. Only a jury of my peers could clear my name. I owed it to myself to continue in the face of the most bizarre and unexpected assaults that one could imagine.

I'll begin with a scheme concocted by the university administration that was a perfect example of the intermingling of their arrogance and deceit.

As I mentioned earlier, after I left the university I was still a member of the community and a fan of the student-athletes and coaches involved in Wolf Pack athletics. And I still attended the games that were open to the public. My presence on campus didn't pose any problem for the administration – other than their guilty consciences. However, unknown to me at the time, as I continued to appear on campus, the administration and some of the university's employees were conspiring to smear my reputation and trample on my First Amendment rights.

Of course, none of what follows was known to me in real time. But when the pieces were put together, the puzzle revealed a disturbing picture of the so-called leaders at this institution of higher learning.

First Attempt

On August 27, 2007, a draft of the exit letter from Groth to me contained the following language:

> If you are wanting to be on campus for any reason, you are to notify the Director of Athletics, Cary Groth, for approval prior to your arrival.

Putting aside the bad grammar, this "draft" was returned from Groth to Gena Jones, HR Assistant Vice President, because Groth was not comfortable with this language. In response, HR deleted the undesirable wording from the actual letter that was presented to me. That they even contemplated such an inane stipulation typified their arrogance and abuse of authority. The University of Nevada, Reno, was a public campus that was supported by taxpayers and I was a taxpayer.

Second Attempt

On October 2nd and 3rd of 2007, Nettie, at the direction of Cindy Fox, solicited manufactured complaints from student-athletes I had coached. The declaration below was provided by a student-athlete who Nettie had telephoned:

In the fall of 2007, I [Student-Athlete #1] was contacted by Antoinette Marjanovic [Nettie]. She asked me if I would send in a written complaint about Terri Patraw. [Nettie] said that Cindy Fox stopped in her office and said if you can get the student athletes to write complaints that Terri's presence makes them uncomfortable we can use those statements to get her banned from campus.

This statement was submitted under the penalty of perjury by a student-athlete with nothing to gain and everything to lose. This statement was also supported by Nettie's phone records and email communications. During the period of October 2-3, 2007, in the middle of the soccer season, Nettie initiated the following calls with my former student-athletes:

```
10/02 12:29 PM   360-███████
10/02 12:30 PM   775-███████
10/02 2:29  PM   775-███████
10/02 2:47  PM   775-███████
10/02 2:48  PM   775-███████
10/02 3:50  PM   775-███████
10/02 5:16  PM   360-███████
10/03 12:14 PM   775-███████
10/03 4:08  PM   949-███████
10/03 4:09  PM   408-███████
10/03 4:19  PM   408-███████
10/03 5:39  PM   775-███████
10/03 5:40  PM   775-███████
10/03 6:46  PM   775-███████
10/03 8:21  PM   949-███████
```

On October 3, 2007, at 8:54 pm, Nettie sent an email with an attachment from Blaine, a student-athlete, to Cindy Fox:

From: Antoinette Marjanovic
Sent: Wednesday, October 3, 2007 8:54 PM

To: Cynthia G Fox
Subject: FW:

Here you go, this is from Blaine and [Student-Athlete #2] should be sending me an e-mail tomorrow.

Antoinette Marjanovic

According to phone records Nettie had been in contact with Blaine twice that day – at 4:09 and 4:19 PM – prior to Blaine sending the email – at 4:49 PM – that Nettie had asked her to write. Nettie had also called Student-Athlete #2 shortly before this email was sent to Cindy Fox. However, Student-Athlete #2, who now lived out of state, did not wind up sending Nettie the email that she was anticipating. Instead, Student-Athlete #2 alerted me to Nettie's actions. Even more revealing, Nettie had appealed to former student-athletes who lived out of state. She was soliciting these student-athletes (current and former) to fabricate evidence that could be used illegally against me – a felony. When I found this out I was, of course, struck by their illicit tactics but I was also shocked by their lack of focus on the team. I guess it was the coach in me, but I was appalled at how Nettie and Cindy had virtually abandoned my former team. Was it any wonder that the team had such disappointing results on the field when both its coach and the executive associate AD were consumed with themselves and an agenda that had nothing to do with the team? Nettie and Cindy sabotaged any chance these young athletes had at success that season while they were obsessed with sabotaging me. I always preached to my student-athletes to 'minimize the drama'. I can only imagine the thoughts that ran through their heads when they saw their interim-head coach – Nettie – creating the drama. This incident showed where the leadership of the university was taking it – in a dark and downward spiral propelled by lies and deception.

I had a policy to never hold meetings with any student-athlete alone. Therefore, I always made sure to have a third party present. This practice protected both me and the student-athletes from any false accusations. Because I always adhered to this policy, it would have been impossible for the student-athletes to make an accusation against me that would stick.

Even though Nettie was aware of this policy, she apparently dismissed it. It was another example of how inept they were in carrying out their campaign of deception. The after-the-fact attempts to create allegations against me confirmed what I already knew . . . that the administration did not have a single student-athlete complaint to use from my entire tenure.

Because Blaine's email did not accuse me of any wrongdoing, the university had no use for it. Her only accusation – that I was contacting student-athletes during the season – was too banal for their purposes. But just for the record, while I certainly had the right, I had not been contacting any of my former students. And the university knew that my phone records and email records supported that. I also did not have any social media accounts so that trail ran cold for them as well. So with a provably false accusation, the university never produced Blaine's email until we forced them to. We later subpoenaed Blaine to appear at a deposition. However, at the direction of the General Counsel's Office, she evaded the subpoena. Having graduated in December, she was able to leave town and we could not compel her to return since she was an out-of-state resident. We were not concerned though – her actions were telling – and with Nettie's email to Cindy Fox along with her phone records and the testimony of other student-athletes, we had plenty to share with a jury. Of course, in front of a jury was the last place the university wanted my case to go. The General Counsel's Office was probably still smarting from the jury's angry reaction to their shameful dishonesty in the Charles Stricker retaliation case.

The student-athletes should be applauded for refusing to be drawn into the administration's deplorable schemes. Of all the dirty tactics they tried against me, this one was the most revolting. To ask this of these young people who entrusted their coaching staff to lead them is unforgivable. Nettie, at the behest of Mary Dugan and Cindy Fox, placed them in an awful situation. Although Nettie had power over them on the field and completely controlled their playing time, they resisted the pressure she was applying to get them to do something they knew was very wrong. A coach represents not only fair play on the field but in life as well. Nettie failed them on both fronts. The student-athletes demonstrated more class and a higher sense of morality and ethics than their two supposed leaders, interim-Coach Antoinette Marjanovic and Executive Associate AD Cindy Fox, put together.

In preparation for this book, I contacted Blaine by phone and by messaging on three separate occasions to give her the opportunity to address her involvement. To date she has declined my offer.

Third Attempt

After she failed – through Nettie – to persuade my former student-athletes to write false complaints against me, on October 17, 2007, General Counsel Mary Dugan offered to settle with my attorney, Marc. Dugan's offer contained the following stipulation:

No appearance on campus.

This meant, of course, that the offer was only good if I agreed to stay off campus. I declined the offer.

After the soccer season ended with a disappointing 6-11-1 record under Nettie and Graeme's leadership, my two former assistant coaches were desperate to retain their coaching jobs. Based on the dismal showing with Nettie at the helm, their prospects were dim. Groth posted the head-coaching job and Nevada was soliciting candidates for the position throughout December with a goal of hiring a new coach in January. It seemed that Nettie's willingness to help the university ruin my reputation hadn't won the day for her yet. So she continued to scheme.

A witness gave the following testimony in a deposition:

Q Did Nettie say that they wanted to ban Ms. Patraw from campus?
A I had heard Nettie and Graeme talking about trying to get Terri banned from campus, yes.
Q Okay. And so you can't tell us whether this declaration accurately reflects that phone call or not, can you?
A . . . She [Nettie] had told me at one point that they were trying to get Terri banned, so I don't remember if that phone call specifically said, If you write this down, we can get her banned.

Fourth attempt

On December 17, 2007, after all the previous attempts to defame me had failed, Nettie and Graeme manufactured their own false written reports about me. Their false reports revealed two conflicting accounts as to what was alleged to have occurred at a basketball game on campus:

According to Graeme's account:

Miss Marjanovic and I **continued to walk towards the exit** without response. Ms. Patraw then stepped towards Miss Marjanovic and **placed her hands** around Miss Marjanovic's shoulder and neck and pulled Miss Marjanovic towards her.

According to Nettie's account:

We were **walking back to the arena and as we turned the corner to the left** I felt **a hand and arm** grab me around my shoulder/neck area trying to yank me back.

Graeme and Nettie failed to get their *stories* straight between just the two of them. They couldn't even coordinate their stories as to whether they were coming or going from the arena. If their statements were true, why didn't Graeme and Nettie go to the police immediately after the game? Why didn't they press charges? The paper trail revealed that they had had a meeting with Associate AD's Cindy Fox and Keith Hackett. On direction from General Counsel Dugan, Cindy and Keith encouraged Graeme and Nettie to write these false statements about interacting with me at a basketball game. After "thinking about it" Graeme and Nettie complied, knowing that Nettie's only chance to secure the head coaching position on a full-time basis likely depended on her cooperation.

I knew nothing about any of this until General Counsel Mary Dugan submitted the manufactured yet conflicting statements in discovery several months later.

Of course I knew these allegations were trumped up. So to prove that they were false, we requested the video surveillance records of this alleged incident via the university's extensive video surveillance system that was installed throughout the campus. Dugan admitted that they could not produce them. A criminal complaint was filed with the UNRPD seeking charges against Graeme and Nettie for fabricating evidence. Officer Warren Conley of the UNRPD stated at the outset that he had immediately recognized that Graeme and Nettie had written conflicting statements about their alleged interaction with me at a basketball game. I also offered to take a polygraph test. While he admitted this was a viable option, he never took me up on it. It was the UNRPD after all and they didn't deal in the truth. Their mission wasn't to expose the lies, but instead was to hide the truth. I explained to him that the paper trail led to Mary Dugan's office and that she was ultimately behind this. Officer Conley refused to interview her. Apparently, the UNR police were not only "intimidating" but were among the "intimidated" themselves. Dugan pulled the strings of the UNRPD. The police did the spying and manufacturing of evidence for her office. Conley knew he could not implicate Dugan or he would lose his job. But he did concede to me that he "*could see what was going on here.*"

Two days after his General Counsel Dugan secured her manufactured evidence, President Glick sent his private police force, the UNRPD, several miles outside its jurisdiction to harass me at home. Glick had them deliver a letter informing me that he was banning me from campus. The letter contained no allegation of any wrongdoing. Drunk on their own sense of power and invincibility, the university administration operated in a culture of disobedience to the law, while trampling on the US Constitution.

Glick cited the NSHE Code (6.5.1 and 6.18) to support his actions. However, those provisions did not apply to me. Code 6.5.1 referred to employees on Administrative Leave. I was not an employee and I was not on leave. Code 6.18 allowed the President to direct a person to leave the campus if the person engaged in prohibited conduct. It said nothing about banning a citizen indefinitely. Nobody has ever produced any evidence that I had engaged in prohibited conduct – all they produced were conflicting lies typed up on a piece of paper that didn't hold up to the light of day. It would be obvious to a ten-year-old that my former assistants were lying. It is indisputable that at least one of them was. Regardless, President Glick had no authority to ban any citizen from campus.

Jeff wrote to Dugan's office:

Please provide an explanation for how President Glick believes that a ban is authorized under one or both of these provisions – NSHE Code (6.5.1 and 6.18) – because my client and I do not see it.

Jeff never received a response. Dugan refused to answer because she had no answer.

Because Glick failed to produce any authority supporting his actions, the campus ban was never honored by me or enforced by them. That did not stop Glick from harassing others though. Glick also issued invalid campus bans against Dr. Hussein and police officer Lane Grow after he fired them, despite knowing he had no such authority. Notably, Glick never banned Rich Merritt from campus despite his and his student-athlete's admission that he had hit the student. Instead Glick kept Merritt employed as Head Coach of the Nevada men's golf team. Who would have dreamed that the physical abuse of student-athletes would provide job security at a Division I university? Glick also allowed professor Robert Karlin freedom to roam the campus, who after he sexually assaulted Dr. Mary Lahren, continued to prey on graduate students while remaining employed at the university.

It is worth noting that Nettie and Graeme were not rewarded for their behavior. Nettie was terminated from her coaching position and both were forced to leave the university. They had to recognize after Nettie's dismissal that they had just been used; like so many other UNR employees, they had been willing pawns entwined in the tangled web of corruption on the UNR campus.

What goes around sometimes does come back around.

CHAPTER 8

Manufacturing Evidence

"Truly, to tell lies is not honorable; but when the truth entails tremendous ruin, to speak dishonorably is pardonable."

~ Sophocles

Jeff cited the above quote from the ancient Greek tragedian Sophocles in an emergency motion filed in court to expose the manufacturing of false evidence by the attorneys for the defense team. Jeff suggested that the university inscribe this quote as a motto on the front of its General Counsel's Office in Reno, Nevada to proclaim that UNR attorneys choose to lie and deceive rather than face the ruination that the truth would bring about. Read on and you'll see how apt the reference is.

NCAA Reports

I had a clean NCAA record, having never been charged with or investigated for violating an NCAA rule for my entire tenure. Through discovery we learned that UNR had a lengthy file detailing NCAA violations committed by other Nevada coaches within the department. It is common for athletic department employees to commit minor NCAA violations due to inadvertence or misunderstanding of the numerous rules and regulations. These are usually harmless infractions and ones that provide no competitive advantage. But some violations are clearly committed with a blatant disregard for the rules.

With NCAA violations being a hot topic in my case – and the file we had secured on other coaches at Nevada who remained employed – UNR attempted to manufacture two NCAA reports on me after I left the university. Since Groth had looked in my personnel file and had nothing to use against me, it was obvious that the defense team was desperate.

Jean Perry, Nevada's Special Assistant for Athletics, Academics, and Compliance, was responsible for overseeing NCAA compliance at Nevada. She testified that her subordinate, Director of Compliance Sandie Niedergall, conducted investigations for the university, and that Sandie "has total authority to consult with whoever she needs and wants to consult with"; and that Sandie "keeps very extensive records."

However, Sandie later testified in a deposition that she was ordered by Perry to charge me with an NCAA violation after I left the university. Sandie was cautioned by Perry not to contact me about it. Sandie stated that this incident was the first during her entire career in which she had been prohibited from talking to the target of an investigation before its completion. The violation cited was petty and inconsequential – it involved whether a visiting recruit slept on or off campus. But neither Sandie nor anyone in compliance interviewed the recruit or me. There was no evidence to support the accusation; it was a clear act of retaliation.

There is more . . . Sandie also testified that she was responsible for conducting investigations of potential NCAA violations at Nevada and that she signed off on all the reports. During her deposition, Jeff produced a copy of another NCAA report that was written up about me after I left the university. It was signed by Dr. Jean Perry. I knew Sandie well and watched her reaction. It was obvious that that moment was the first time she had laid eyes on the report. She was stunned and her face turned several shades of red. My attorney asked Sandie why she hadn't signed that particular report. Sandie appeared visibly shaken by what was unfolding before her. She said that she had never seen the report before and was surprised to see that Perry had signed it. In the report, Perry indicated that she worked with Cindy and Cary on it. These three senior administrators had concealed this report from Sandie, the very person responsible for conducting investigations and signing off on the reports. General Counsel Dugan squirmed in her chair as she watched Sandie's deposition unfold.

In this report, Jean Perry, with the help of her co-conspirators –
Cindy Fox and Cary Groth – attempted to charge me with failing to
report all NCAA violations that I was aware of. However, in a deposition
after they manufactured this report, Groth was questioned about it. She
testified as follows:

> I'm not so sure what Terri failed to do. I mean, if there were no
> allegations, she had no obligation to report those. If there were
> allegations, she did. I can't tell you if she had any.

Which was it? It seems Groth could not keep her story straight. Her
testimony is a clear admission that they fabricated this report against me
without basis, and certainly without due process. Cary, Cindy and Jean
manufactured this report the day after they learned that the university
was under investigation by the NCAA. Panic ensued and damage control
was underway. Jean Perry had submitted this report to the NCAA while
the NCAA was investigating Head Golf Coach Rich Merritt, clearly
intent on discrediting me and covering the administration's backside.
There will be more on the NCAA's investigation of the University of
Nevada later.

Jeff and I notified the NCAA of this act of fraud committed by Jean,
Cindy, and Cary, including how they had colluded to conceal it from
Sandie, the person responsible for such reporting. The NCAA did not
charge me with any violations. Sandie left the university not long after
her deposition. Jean Perry remains the Special Assistant for Athletics,
Academics, and Compliance at Nevada.

University of Nevada Personnel File

There can be no greater admission of guilt in an employment dispute
than the employer's submission of fabricated personnel evaluations. The
university lawyers shamelessly attempted to submit a falsified version
of my personnel evaluation from 2005 at my reinstatement hearing.
Despite having been caught red-handed there and forced to withdraw
it from evidence, they tried the same despicable act in the district court.
The district court judge recognized that it was not a legitimate evaluation
but failed to sanction the university lawyers for committing fraud in his
court.

During my three-plus years at Nevada, I received "commendable" evaluations. My supervisor, Cindy Fox, testified that "commendable" was the highest possible rating available and therefore it spoke for itself. The 2005 evaluation was changed to "satisfactory." Document #1739, listed below, was the falsified document that was signed by Cindy Fox and submitted by the UNR lawyers. The actual evaluations, submitted by the university human resources office, are also listed below with court identification numbers, and had been signed by my supervisor, the athletic director, and the university president.

Fraudulent Personnel Evaluation Submitted by UNR Attorneys
2005 "Satisfactory" – Document #1739

Actual Personnel Evaluations Submitted by Human Resources
2005 "Commendable" – Document #000057
2006 "Commendable" – Document #000051
2007 "Commendable" – Document #000043

The university defined a "commendable" evaluation as having "successfully met, and in some areas, significantly exceeded established goals and objectives." It also denoted the "achievement of high levels of productivity and competence." Team Dugan could not let that stand and twice attempted to insert a fraudulent evaluation of my performance.

Administrative Assistant to the Athletics Director

UNR was indefatigable in their pursuit of something, anything they could use against me to sully my name and attack my credibility. Throughout the discovery process, Dugan and her underlings would routinely send over piles of documents. Although most of it was just an assault on trees, there were usually a few nuggets that we found interesting. One such document was an email communication from Cary and Cindy's administrative assistant, Andrea Pearson, to the US Soccer Federation, the national governing body of soccer.

Andrea's email was an attempt to gather 'negative information' about me after I had left the university. Andrea wrote in an email to the soccer organization that the university wanted to acquire information on me as they were considering hiring me. Well that was certainly a lie. Andrea and her husband had been friends of mine. I had eaten dinner at their home and attended their five-year-old son's soccer games. But the employees, just like the student-athletes, were put in untenable positions by their supervisors Cary and Cindy.

The soccer organization confirmed that I had received my USSF National "A" license just as I had listed on my resume. Andrea's efforts to dig up dirt on me had failed.

Former Assistant Basketball Coach

Another nugget was discovered in an email sent by Dedrique, the former Nevada assistant basketball coach I had dated, to Groth:

Can you remind me again what the email I need to say to you needs to have in it? I want to make sure I am sending the right email. Thanks

An hour later, at the direction of Groth, he sent an email asking her to assist in seeing to it that I "cease all communication with him." Groth, an athletic director at an NCAA Division I institution, used her position of power to coerce others into committing fraud. She was so desperate to smear me that she committed crimes using her university issued email account. Her desperation and self-serving motives were exposed in these communications. Dedrique later in a letter to the university administration recanted his false accusation and apologized for any harm that he caused me.

Former Assistant Soccer Coach

Over time I began to realize just how utterly dishonest the UNR legal team was. But I also realized they were not the sharpest tools in the shed. Knowing that my former assistant – Graeme – was working at the University of Oklahoma after he left Nevada, going on a hunch, we submitted a Freedom of Information Act (FOIA) request to the University of Oklahoma. Most documents at public institutions, including emails, are considered open records.

In the FOIA request to the University of Oklahoma, we asked for all email communications between Graeme and the University of Nevada lawyers and certain other UNR employees. While the request was pending, I received a letter in the mail from a staff attorney at Oklahoma. It was a letter addressed to Mary Dugan, UNR General Counsel, and courtesy copied to me. The letter notified Dugan that her request for Oklahoma to withhold records responsive to my request was denied.

Dugan, a University of Nevada attorney, was trying to assert an attorney-client privilege over a University of Oklahoma employee (Graeme) – which is every bit as absurd as it sounds. The attorney at Oklahoma told her that they were unable to assert that privilege for her and that Dugan would have to take the matter up in an Oklahoma court if she wanted to restrict my FOIA request.

Graeme must have been made aware of our FOIA request by the Oklahoma attorney and subsequently notified Mary Dugan, who then tried to intervene, of course, without our knowledge. Much to Dugan's chagrin, her efforts to derail the FOIA request had been relayed to me when the Oklahoma attorney copied me on her response to Dugan. Dugan's outrageous attempt to assert privilege made clear that she and Graeme had something to hide. Dugan did not go to the Oklahoma courts with her frivolous argument and the requested documents arrived from Oklahoma shortly thereafter.

The documents revealed the following:

On November 16, 2009, the soccer coach who had replaced me resigned from Nevada after two seasons. Graeme contacted former colleagues in the Nevada athletic department the same day and attempted to secure support for the open head coaching position. He asked one employee "Who'd be my allies in the dept?"

On December 8, 2009, Graeme emailed Groth about the head coaching position. Shortly thereafter, a flurry of email communications was sent between Dugan's subordinate Charles Hilsabeck and Graeme. Hilsabeck offered to fly Graeme to Reno so that he could assist them in their efforts against me. Graeme was the perfect pawn. Based on his quest to procure the head coaching position that had been vacated, it was obvious that he would say "yes" to just about anything. Graeme agreed to help them.

The lawyers said that they wanted to fly him in, so that "we can work with you to prepare you." They also discussed arrangements for a telephone call between UNR's private attorney Kent Robison, the master of malfeasance, and Graeme to "work on" Graeme's testimony.

On January 21, 2010, after several back and forth emails to arrange Graeme's flight to Reno, Groth named a new soccer coach. Despite his agreement to assist Groth and Dugan's team in their games of fraud and lies, Graeme was not named the new coach. In fact, he was not even given an on-campus interview. He had to feel the sting of having been exploited so blatantly with not even the pretense that he had a chance for the coaching position.

It was the same M.O. that Groth had used with Nettie when Nettie was instructed to solicit student-athletes to fabricate complaints against me. Shortly after she had done their dirty deeds for them, they fired Nettie from her coaching position. Graeme was apparently not paying attention when Nettie had been used so shamelessly.

On January 29, 2010, Graeme sent an email to Hilsabeck notifying him that he could no longer fly into town to assist them; his motives revealed.

I gave Graeme his first NCAA Division I coaching job. My last personal interaction with him was on the golf course one week before I left the university. He had vowed his support and loyalty to me when he declared that he would want to follow me to Wisconsin, if I were to seek the position there. But his loyalty was just a veneer. He later showed his true character; that he would do and say anything to advance his career no matter how devastating his actions would be to me.

Solicitation of Student-Athletes

Dugan's attempt to co-opt Graeme was reminiscent of the solicitation of false evidence from the student-athletes after I left the university. This declaration from a student-athlete bears repeating:

In the fall of 2007, I [Student-Athlete #1] was contacted by Antoinette Marjanovic [Nettie]. She asked me if I would send in a written complaint about Terri Patraw. [Nettie] said that Cindy Fox stopped in her office and said if you can get the student athletes to write complaints that Terri's presence makes them uncomfortable we can use those statements to get her banned from campus.

Cindy and Cary were aware of the positive remarks I had received from my student-athletes in the anonymous surveys that the administration conducted after each season. Graeme and Nettie had worked with me every day. Yet they had nothing to offer the university to use against me. After I left Nevada, Dugan had the university IT department access the computer I had used for the 3.5 years I was at the university. Although they tried, they could not find a single negative file or email to help their cause.

Arizona State University Personnel File

After my interview with Nevada back in 2004, I had offered to provide my personnel files from my tenure as a head soccer coach at Arizona State University. Two days after my interview for the position at Nevada I sent this email to Cindy Fox:

From: Terri Patraw
Sent: Sunday, January, 2004 8:02 PM
To: Cindy Fox
Subject: soccer interview

Cindy, thank you for a wonderful visit to Nevada on Friday . . . I also wanted to offer you a release of my ASU personnel file if that would help support my tenure there.

Sincerely,
Terri Patraw

Leif Reid, son of US Senate Majority Leader Harry Reid and Cindy Fox's personal attorney, produced this email during discovery. It was submitted as document D-Fox 00274. Submission of this communication indicated that Leif and Cindy were well aware that the university had been granted full access to my ASU file in 2004. Of course Cindy – having chaired the committee that had hired me – had obviously referenced me with ASU administrators. Cindy had even shared with me that a former ASU athletic director, upon learning of my appointment at Nevada, had told her that she made "a great hire." With this information, the following account is even more troubling.

After my claims against the university were initiated in late 2007, I contacted Arizona State University to secure access to my personnel files. I was encouraged by Dr. Hussein to get my personnel files from all previous employers. He based his advice on his own experience with the university, knowing that Mary Dugan would go to any lengths to defame and defeat me. And manipulation of my personnel records would not be beyond the realm of possibility. Being a jump ahead of them and procuring my files would be a way to protect myself. I learned just how right Dr. Hussein was.

Despite my repeated attempts to get my files from all three universities where I had been previously employed, I came up empty. They all had retention policies of five years or less and I was eight years removed from ASU, my most recent employer, at the time. It should be noted that if UNR had responded to my offer to provide my ASU files in 2004, they could have had them – ASU's retention policy was five years – and my voluntary offer made clear that I had nothing to hide.

Dugan didn't have any better luck getting my file from my former employer, Arizona State University, than I did. There weren't any files to be had, of course, but that didn't stop them. They were very resourceful and came up with a voluminous stack of documents on ASU letterhead. How on earth did they get their hands on my own personnel file that I wasn't able to obtain and, in fact, didn't even exist?! The answer was, they manufactured a personnel file that was not really a personnel file at all. The stack of documents consisted primarily of policies and procedures for ASU human resources – which even mentioned the five-year retention policy. Oddly, it also included an alleged personnel file of an individual that I had never worked with. There were also some random handwritten notes that were neither addressed to nor signed by anyone. This was clearly another rushed and desperate intimidation tactic.

These documents were produced in the spring of 2009, just days before trial, when the huge stack was dropped by Robison on the table in front of me at my final deposition. If this dramatic introduction of new documents was orchestrated to elicit a reaction from me, the attorneys left disappointed. I was experienced enough by then in their fraudulent schemes that I remained unfazed, and the deposition was uneventful. After learning about this despicable act of deception, Jeff filed an emergency motion for sanctions against the defendants, all the usual suspects: Cary Groth, Milton Glick, and the Nevada System of

Higher Education. Jeff asked for sanctions against the defendants and their unscrupulous defense team, which included some names that are probably familiar to you by now – Dugan, Robison, Hilsabeck, and Arrascada – and some new attorneys – Leif Reid and Stacy Luedtke. As it turned out, the new attorneys were of the same ilk as the others. The sanctions were sought against these individuals for committing fraud against me and against the court. Arizona State University was listed in our motion as complicit in the commission of the fraud by its providing false documents with the university's imprimatur.

The emergency motion read in part:

The conduct described herein demonstrates . . . deceit and fraud upon the court and Plaintiff. The conspiracy involved coordination between two academic institutions and a large number of attorneys to obtain documents under false pretense to harass and intimidate Plaintiff . . . .

UNR President Milton Glick had been the Provost at Arizona State University for many years but was finally let go and then hired by UNR. He fielded lawsuits at ASU and therefore had cause to be in close contact with ASU Associate General Counsel Cynthia Jewett even after he left ASU. So it would be a stretch to believe that Glick, or his staff, had nothing to do with procuring these fraudulent files from the General Counsel's office at ASU. Glick was not a newcomer to retaliation cases. He was named as a defendant in a retaliation lawsuit at Arizona State by cancer researcher Bob Pettit, one of the top organic chemists in the world. Pettit's cancer research is recognized as some of the most groundbreaking ever, resulting in 65 patents on anti-cancer compounds at ASU. But Pettit alleged that he was fired in retaliation for blowing the whistle at ASU. The lawsuit from ASU followed Glick to UNR and he was still fighting it up until his death in 2011. Glick's long struggle with the Pettit lawsuit kept him in close contact with Jewett. It was Glick's ongoing relationship with Cynthia Jewett, ASU legal counsel, through the Pettit-ASU litigation that garnered her cooperation with UNR.

It is worth noting that on January 30, 2009, ESPN reported a "landmark settlement" in an Arizona State University rape case:

The settlement comes after the victim and her attorneys completed an exhaustive investigation of ASU's actions before and after the rape, an investigation that her attorneys say revealed previous sexual misconduct by [ASU football player Darnel] Henderson, deletions of important e-mails, destruction of critical documents and false testimony . . . ASU had destroyed records of Henderson's misconduct during the Summer Bridge program, and significant e-mails had been deleted even though ASU knew the victim was about to file suit.

The ASU General Counsel's Office that orchestrated the fraud in this troubling rape case is the same office that corroborated with the UNR General Counsel's Office to submit falsified evidence in my case. Unabashed by the national media exposure of the ASU legal counsel's criminal activity in the rape case, ASU Associate General Counsel Cynthia Jewett sent fraudulent documents to UNR less than two months later.

Receipts indicated that on March 13, 2009, Cynthia Jewett FedExed a package of documents to UNR General Counsel Mary Dugan in Reno, NV. What's very interesting about the date on which this packet was sent is that it was *before* a subpoena was issued and served to ASU General Counsel. Unless Jewett had psychic powers, the only conclusion that one can draw is that there was conversation between Jewett and someone – Mary Dugan or Milton Glick, perhaps, or a private attorney – to coordinate the transmittal of these falsified documents. Further, Jewett was in violation of the subpoena instructions by sending the material directly to Dugan in Reno. The subpoena ordered that the documents requested be presented to a Phoenix law firm, Lewis & Roca LLP – Reid and Luedtke's firm.

The cart was already before the horse when on that same date – March 13, 2009 – attorney Arrascada, on behalf of his client, Cary Groth, requested the Superior Court of the State of Arizona, County of Maricopa, for a subpoena for production of these documents – which were already heading west on a FedEx truck. Arrascada's filing in the Nevada district court said that the out-of-state subpoena was to be served on Jewett – who had already sent the documents on that FedEx truck.

FedEx	Invoice Number	Invoice Date	Account Number
	9-153-35309	April 10, 2009	1088-7450-3
Dropped off:	March 13, 2009		
Automation	INET	Sender	Recipient
Tracking ID	796428571164	Suzanne Copeland	Mary Phelps Dugan, Gen'l Coun
Service Type	Priority Overnight	ASU/General Counsel	University of Nevada-Reno
Package Type	FedEx Pak	300 E. University Dr.	2601 ENTERPRISE RD
Zone	05	TEMPE, AZ 85287	RENO, NV 89512
Packages	1		
Rated Weight	2.0 lbs, 0.9 kgs		
Delivered	March 16, 2009		

On March 16, 2009, Leif Reid's associate at his Arizona office, Stacy Luedtke, applied for issuance of the subpoena in the Superior Court of Arizona on behalf of their client, Cindy Fox. The subpoena that Arrascada had requested in Nevada had to be domesticated in the state of Arizona.

YOU ARE COMMANDED to appear at the time and place specified below to be examined on deposition for the purpose of production of documents by the Defendant Cindy Fox in the above-entitled case . . .

DATE AND TIME OF PERSONAL
APPEARANCE FOR
DEPOSITION: March 30, 2009 at 9:00 am

BEFORE WHOM APPEARANCE
TO BE MADE: Court Reporter

PLACE OF PERSONAL
APPEARANCE

Lewis & Roca LLP
40 N. Central Ave
Phoenix, Arizona 85004

According to the subpoena, ASU was commanded to produce the documents to Lewis & Roca LLP in Phoenix, Arizona on March 30, 2009. But the FedEx receipt says the documents had already been delivered to Mary Dugan in Reno, Nevada – on March 16, 2009.

In simple terms, Jewett produced these fraudulent personnel files and sent them to UNR WITHOUT a subpoena. The lawyers continued to amaze. They were deceptive – but careless in their deceit. They left a trail of incompetence behind them like cookie crumbs that a child could follow.

The twisted tale of the fraudulent personnel files didn't end with the manufacturing of these files. Cindy Fox and President Milton Glick had been added as defendants in my case in April 2008. But on January 22, 2009, through my attorney, I signed a stipulation dismissing Cindy Fox from the lawsuit with prejudice.

Leif Reid had represented Cindy Fox's interest when she was listed as a defendant. Of course, once removed by the judge, she and attorney Reid had no standing in the case. Here is the accurate case caption listing the parties in the case in March 2009, in the midst of the ASU scheme:

TERRI PATRAW,

Plaintiff,

vs.

CARY GROTH, an individual; NEVADA SYSTEM OF HIGHER EDUCATION, a state entity; MILTON GLICK, an individual

Defendants

But this is the caption that was used by Attorneys Reid and Luedtke in the Arizona court for the subpoena:

TERRI PATRAW

Plaintiff

vs.

CARY GROTH, an individual; NEVADA SYSTEM OF HIGHER EDUCATION, a state entity; **CINDY FOX, an individual**, MILTON GLICK, an individual

Defendants

To carry out the fraud, Cindy Fox reappeared in my case, fraudulently listing herself as a defendant, 53 days after I had dismissed her. Cindy was not party to the lawsuit. Her lack of standing made it impossible for her or her attorneys to seek a subpoena for documents to be submitted as evidence in this case – impossible unless rules, regulations and laws were deliberately disregarded. The law was apparently just an unimportant technicality to the defending attorneys. Reid and Luedtke took care of the minor obstacle of no standing by falsifying several court documents to include Cindy Fox's name as a defendant in the case.

Since Reid's law firm had an office in Arizona, it facilitated Dugan's efforts to procure the falsified documents on ASU letterhead from ASU. Despite the fact that Reid no longer had any connection to the case, he requested the subpoena from the Arizona court by filing papers indicating that he was representing one of the defendants in the case, one Cindy Fox. But Cindy wasn't just an innocent pawn in this action. She had self-interest and personal reasons to keep this case from going to trial. She was aware that her husband's conduct during his tenure as head basketball coach was going to be addressed at trial. Additionally, witnesses would be testifying about Cindy's actions, including her witness tampering and solicitation of the student-athletes to fabricate complaints.

Jeff pleaded with the court to invoke its inherent powers to sanction the defense team for its fraud upon the court. In addition to a wide range of sanctions proposed, Jeff, emphasized a preferred and justifiable remedy – that was supported by established case law:

. . . stern measures are the medicine for this high level of judicial deception. The Court should empanel the jury to hear evidence of damages and punitive damages and enter default judgment thereon.

Leif Reid, having committed undeniable fraud upon the court, characterized his action in seeking an illegal subpoena on behalf of a fictitious defendant as a "mistake." That absurd "explanation" did not hold up to scrutiny because Reid himself had no standing to file documents in the case. How does an attorney "mistakenly" appear in a case? The affidavit Reid filed in response to Jeff's motion was not signed under the penalty of perjury. As an attorney, Reid knew that and was purposefully careful in omitting a declaratory statement under oath in the face of the glaring fraud he had committed. He hoped nobody would notice his continued judicial deception, but we did. Without a signature under the penalty of perjury, Reid's affidavit was meaningless.

Jeff had never received notice of the subpoena, which was required by law. The copy of the subpoena that was belatedly produced among the large stack of fabricated documents was curiously unsigned. In other words, there was likely never a subpoena issued, just the appearance of one in an attempt to legitimize the documents.

The evidence proved that the package of "personnel files" from ASU was sent via FedEx before a subpoena was issued. Although the subpoena had been procured by a law firm in Arizona, Jewett sent the material to legal counsel at UNR. Why? They hadn't officially sought the material through subpoena – Leif Reid had through the Arizona law firm. There was obvious collusion in both obtaining the subpoena and in deciding where the documents were to be sent.

On April 1, 2009, Jeff sent a letter to Jewett regarding her unlawful conduct. On April 2, 2009, Jewett responded to Jeff, cc'ing all the attorneys who had standing in my case. Jewett did not include Cindy Fox's attorneys Leif Reid or Stacy Luedtke on the cc list. Even though the subpoena – that Jewett claims was served on her – was issued by Reid and Luedtke, Jewett omitted them from the letter addressing it. That fact shows that Jewett knew that Reid and Luedtke had no standing in the case.

The request for the subpoena and the rapid dispatch of the documentation was all done hastily on the eve of trial. There did not appear to be a whole lot of planning as they did a very poor job of covering their tracks. Deceit doesn't take brilliance it just takes desperation.

Nobody at ASU could or would authenticate the documents – sign an affidavit under the penalty of perjury declaring that the documents at issue were true and correct copies of what they purported to be – despite our challenges for them to do so. All documents at this stage of the litigation had to be authenticated. But even Jewett, with her track record of deceit, wasn't willing to go that far.

But after we presented all this indisputable evidence of mail fraud and falsification of court documents, on May 5, 2009, the presiding judge of the Second Judicial District Court of the State of Nevada in and for the county of Washoe, denied our request for sanctions. The sum total of his decision was one word: "Denied." We were not privy to the reasons for the judge's decision. Let me introduce you to the judge in question – Judge Patrick Flanagan. He will surface again

*   *   *

This entire after-the-fact attempt to "create" evidence is demonstrative of UNR's lack of any defense or case against me. As Groth admitted, "Terri, you're a great, great coach. Nobody can deny that. I just need to move on. I looked in your personnel file. There was nothing to use against you." In spite of this brief, unguarded flash of honesty, the university administration literally spent years attempting to fabricate after-the-fact justifications to smear my name and reputation and all because I had looked out for the university and protected the student-athletes.

There are a lot of hard lessons learned in life. One lesson I learned during this phase of my experience was just how easy it is to fabricate documents and emails with just a few clicks of the mouse and a few clean copies from a photocopy machine. But this fraud was not isolated to me. In Dr. Hussein's case, the UNR lawyers – led by Dugan – relied on a published book to defeat one of his retaliation claims against the university. The book, the "Guide for the Care and Use of Agricultural Animals in Agricultural Research and Teaching", was published by the Federation of Animal Science Societies, a US society promoting animal agriculture located in Illinois. Team Dugan removed the copyright page to conceal their fraud, made a photocopy of the book, submitted it to a federal judge, and insisted that it was a UNR guide that was authored by the University of Nevada's "Institutional Animal Care and Use Committee" (IACUC). The IACUC consisted of three faculty members in Dr. Hussein's department that had never produced a book in their lifetime.

It should be stipulated that these levels of deception by attorneys representing the University of Nevada, Reno occur when "the truth entails tremendous ruin."

CHAPTER 9

Witness Tampering

"If you want to control someone, all you have to do is make them feel afraid."

~ Paulo Coelho

The university administration exercised control over nearly all witnesses because most witnesses were either employed by them or were students at the university. The sheer disparity of power and position was a silent message that cooperation and support was expected from those who were called as witnesses. Led by General Counsel Mary Dugan, the university lawyers' modus operandi was to call the employees who were under subpoena to the legal counsel's office to discuss their testimony days before their depositions. Merely telling the truth doesn't generally require such prompting or practice. But Dugan had to establish in advance which witnesses could be coerced to lie and which ones were more amenable to the "I cannot recall" strategy. During the deposition, Dugan stationed herself or one of her underlings directly beside the witnesses and focused upon them with great intensity. Even though the witnesses did not ask for representation nor need it, Dugan appointed herself as counsel to anyone under subpoena . . . whether they wanted her or not. I was of course present at all the depositions and each time observed that Dugan or her underlings met with these witnesses both prior to and during breaks at the proceedings. Knowing most of the witnesses on a personal and professional level, I could sense by their initial interaction with me just how forthcoming they were going to be under oath.

The intimidation tactics that Dugan employed to influence testimony took on several forms. The following schemes demonstrate the lengths they went to in an effort to obstruct justice at this taxpayer-funded institution of higher learning.

Fearing the testimony of the student-athletes, the university subpoenaed one to a deposition in Robison's office approximately a month before trial. Glick and Dugan employed their private police force to intimidate the student at the very outset. Dugan had the student-athlete served with a subpoena by a university police officer at a local Starbucks. This action was an illegal service since parties to an action are restricted from executing the service of subpoenas on behalf of their own case preparation and litigation. But Dugan and other UNR attorneys showed their belief that rules and even laws didn't apply to them. I can just imagine how a young female student felt when she was handed a subpoena by an armed, uniformed cop. Of course she had no idea it was an illegal service. But the message was crystal clear – cooperation was not only sought, it was expected.

After serving her with the subpoena at Starbucks, the UNR police officer invited the student-athlete to have coffee with him, bought her coffee, and attempted to discuss her involvement in the case. His discussion of the case was completely inappropriate. Clearly he was sent to influence this student-athlete by General Counsel Dugan and her minions. I had never heard of this officer nor had the student-athlete. How did he know enough about the case to even attempt to discuss it with the student? Obviously Dugan and her staff had prepped him, and expressed their concern about this student's knowledge. However, like so many of their other attempts to rig the process, these efforts failed as well. Oh, and how they did fail! While I was pained that this student-athlete had to be subjected to this mess, I have to admit that I could not have been prouder of her. Her testimony was strong, powerful, and courageous, despite UNR's private attorney Kent Robison doing everything he could to rattle her, manipulate her testimony and twist her words. He tried every lawyer trick in the book against this young witness, but hit a roadblock at every turn. Even the court reporter could not repress a smile when the student-athlete knocked Robison back on his heels time and time again. The so-called "super lawyer" finally gave up red-faced, steam emanating from his bald head. Robison despised anyone who spoke the truth, and this witness was as compelling and articulate as they come. After her deposition, the university officials certainly recognized that this student-athlete's testimony would be compelling to a jury. It strengthened their resolve that this case could never go to trial. This one young student alone could bury them.

As was explained in an earlier chapter, Cindy Fox conspired with Assistant Coach Antoinette Marjanovic to solicit manufactured complaints from student-athletes.

Cindy and Cary also attempted to defame me and tamper with potential witnesses by sharing fabricated documents with my former student-athletes and colleagues.

Student-Athlete Deposition:

Q And why did you send that email or text message?
A Because I had been up in the athletic department with Cindy [Fox] and Cary [Groth], I had been up there a lot because I was intrigued with what was going on. And one day they [Cindy and Cary] said, if you really want to know everything, here you go. And they handed me a big stack of papers about the case.

Cindy had also given money and offered free basketball tickets to a key on-campus witness just minutes prior to the witness's deposition. Cindy later engaged in a screaming tirade in the witness's office after Jeff had exposed Cindy's offer of money and freebies. Because of Cindy's flagrant behavior, all athletic department employees were restricted from entering the Office of Prospective Students – where this particular employee was assigned – even if they needed to conduct university business. Athletic department personnel were forced to wait and meet with their contacts at the front desk of this on-campus department. This draconian restriction signaled the frustration of other university employees in having to deal with Cary and Cindy who were being viewed with growing distrust. Cindy's behavior was a tacit acknowledgement of her guilt. It was becoming obvious that Cary and Cindy were putting their own concerns above those of the university. Their crusade to cover themselves and strike back at me was creating tension and placing obstacles in the way of other employees in the fulfillment of their responsibilities. Cindy's outburst at this employee indicated she was terrified that the information the employee possessed would prove to be adverse to the university as well as to Cary and Cindy.

Further evidence of tampering by Cary, Cindy, and others was revealed at the deposition of this same university employee:

Q Did Cary Groth ever call you and encourage you to stay out of this lawsuit?

A Yes, she – yes, she did.

Q Did Cindy Fox ever call you and encourage you to stay out of this lawsuit?

A Yes, she did.

Q Did Golf Coach Rich Merritt ever call you and encourage you to stay out of this lawsuit?

A Yes, he did.

Q You mentioned that, you said Cary Groth called you regarding Terri Patraw's lawsuit?

A Yes.

Q Okay. And regarding the telephone conversation, you have told us everything that she [Cary Groth] said to you to your recollection?

A . . . [Groth] just said, you know, you are going to want to stay, keep your mouth shut, stay quiet, you know, stay out of this because it's going to involve attorneys and you, to protect your family, you don't want to be involved.

Q Okay. Continue. What else did [Cindy Fox] say?

A Just, you know, to, again the same thing that Cary did, just stay out of it. You know, you will want to protect your family and protect those boys. And just, you know, to remain quiet. Don't talk to Terri. You know, those types of things.

Q Did anybody ever say to you that Terri wasn't your friend?

A Yes.

Q Who?

A Cindy Fox.

Q When was that, do you remember? Was it after the violations came out?

A Yeah, yeah. She [Cindy] had called my house.

Q Cindy had?

A   Uh-huh (affirmative).

Q   Did you say anything else in that call?

A   For the most part I just tried to listen as much as I could. She told me that, not to trust Terri. That Terri would, she is not your friend like you think she is. She is not a trustworthy individual. I pretty much kind of questioned her because they [Cindy and Terri] were so close that, you know, I mean, they were always at the games together. I mean, you saw them together quite a lot. She [Cindy] was always having me go to Terri for everything, you know, so I kind of questioned her in the sense of, you know, why would you have me go to somebody that's not trustworthy? And, you know, and I also said to her at the time, I said, that's funny because I always kind of pictured Terri as the poster child of athletics. I mean, she was on every committee, she, anybody that got hired, she was on the committee. She was on my hiring committee. So I just – I was kind of shocked by that statement, and –

Q   By the way, in that earlier discussion that Cindy had asked you about the violations?

A   In her office?

Q   Yeah. Didn't she tell you that she thought that Terri was honest?

A   Yeah.

Q   Okay. So now she is telling you something different in the phone call; is that correct?

A   Yes.

Q   Did you write a personal statement on this [office] incident with Cindy Fox?

A   I did, yeah. It was in here.

Q   Why did you do that?

A   I was, after the incident, I was told pretty much by everybody, by my attorney, by my immediate supervisor, as well as his supervisor, that I, you know, had two choices: To either write a personal statement, or I needed to go fill out a harassment claim on both Jean Perry and Cindy Fox.

Absent any defense to my allegations, the university went to great lengths to obstruct justice, while creating hostile environments for both the students and employees. This was not the education that the students sought when they enrolled at the University of Nevada, Reno. The harder the defense team worked to conceal the truth by silencing me, repressing evidence and tampering with witnesses, the deeper the hole they dug for themselves. They didn't learn the lesson of the old adage: when you find yourself in a hole . . . stop digging.

So, the question lingered . . . just who was going to dig them out?

CHAPTER 10

Lies, Lies, and Damn Lies

"There are some things one remembers even though they may never have happened."

~ Harold Pinter

There were essentially four issues that my case was centered on: 1) Did Groth, as the university's athletic director, react appropriately to reports of NCAA and Title IX violations in her department; 2) Did she offer me a contract on August 22, 2007, just six days before I left Nevada; 3) How was I rated on my annual personnel evaluations; and 4) Did Groth have cause for ending my Nevada tenure. Despite the years of litigation that I was forced to endure, the entire case boiled down to these salient points. These fundamental questions represented what would be presented to a judge and jury for resolution.

*   *   *

During discovery, yet another email came into our possession. The email, dated June 22, 2006, was sent to Groth from a campus official and referred to allegations of NCAA violations in the Nevada men's basketball program. Knowing that Groth had done everything she could to protect Rich Merritt despite his significant violations in the golf program, Jeff asked her how she had responded to this June 22, 2006, email referencing basketball violations a year earlier:

Q Did you take it to [Director of Compliance Sandie] Niedergall?
A I didn't.
Q Did you tell [Faculty Athletic Representative] Jean Perry about it?
A She was – *Jean Perry wasn't hired at the time.*
Q So it was just Sandie on the Board?
A No, *our faculty athletics rep at the time was Chris Exline, and I showed him this letter,* and I can't tell you exactly from that time on
Q Do you know if you did anything at all with –
A *No. I don't know if he had a conversation with her or not.*

Groth lied under oath three times in this exchange: 1) Jean Perry was hired on January 1, 2006. She had been on board for six months at the time Groth received the email; 2) Dr. Chris Exline had passed away on April 11, 2006, two months before the existence of the June 22, 2006 email. Groth did not and could not "show him this letter"; and 3) Groth knew that Exline did not have any "conversations" with anyone about the email since he didn't receive the email and was, in fact, deceased. His distinguished career was recognized in an April 13, 2006, article about his passing:

Chris Exline, a beloved geography professor in the College of Science and, for many at the University of Nevada, Reno, one of the most familiar faces on campus, died April 11, 2006 at his Sparks home. He was 58 *(McDonnell).*

Not only did Groth conceal this email from the top NCAA compliance official on campus – Jean Perry – Groth admitted in her testimony that she concealed it from the Director of Compliance, Sandie Niedergall. Both Sandie and Jean confirmed that Groth had not informed them about it. One would think that revelations about the wrongdoing of the university's athletic director (i.e., her failure to investigate or report NCAA violations) would result in her suspension or even dismissal. But that wasn't the case. President Glick made clear time and time again that education, student welfare and, indeed, the university's mission statement, were secondary to protecting his retaliatory administration.

But Groth's false testimony was not an inadvertent mistake. Groth's aversion to addressing allegations of NCAA violations in her department was demonstrated not only by her continued employment of Golf Coach Merritt and her retaliation against me, but in her cover-up of this June 2006 email – which referenced allegations of NCAA violations in her biggest revenue-generating sport. We did not immediately call Groth out on her lies. So, in an effort to demonstrate that Groth handled this report of NCAA violations properly, UNR Assistant General Counsel Charles Hilsabeck asked Groth about the June 2006 email again twelve days later, on February 11, 2008:

Q   Okay. What did you do about it?
A   I went down talked to [Head Basketball Coach] Mark Fox, asked him if he was aware of them. He didn't know anything about it, *called Dedrique, asked him*, and then *had a conversation with our faculty rep*, and I don't know what he did about it.
Q   Who is the faculty rep?
A   *It's Dr. Exline, Chris Exline.*

Groth reaffirmed her *story* in this follow-up deposition. But she knew she did not "have a conversation with our faculty rep . . . Dr. Exline." If she did, it had to be at a séance. Adding to her problems, Dedrique would later state that Groth did not call him, and UNR admitted that it could not produce a billing record of the alleged long-distance phone call between Groth and Dedrique.

The university lawyers were complicit, having assisted Groth in covering up her cover-up. Revealing just how low they were willing to stoop, just days after Groth lied under oath about turning over the allegations to Exline, his obituary was removed from the university website. Unknown to Groth and the UNR lawyers, we had already printed a copy and it was part of our growing pile of evidence. Groth was clearly living the mantra that if you repeat a lie often enough, it becomes the truth. But the defense team's power of deceit had its limitations: there was no escaping Groth's inescapable perjury.

Groth was not done with her lies about her claim that she turned over the report of NCAA violations in the men's basketball program to Exline. She faced the same questions from the NCAA just three weeks after giving her false testimony in the depositions. What Groth did not know at the time was that the NCAA already had a copy of Exline's obituary and was apprised of her false testimony at the two depositions. So without this knowledge, Groth continued weaving her web of lies, with only a slight alteration. She told the NCAA that *she recalled having a conversation with Dr. Exline* about the June 2006 email. However, she *did not recall contacting Dedrique directly, but she believed Mark Fox contacted him.* Dedrique, however, said that neither Groth nor Mark Fox contacted him. The bigger the conspiracy and the more people involved in an act of deceit, the more difficult it is to control the message.

Jean Perry testified that administrators who were aware of allegations of NCAA violations had an obligation to report them. Sandie Niedergall said that it was the rules and requirements, as well as the ethics of the department to bring forth any allegations. According to NCAA Bylaw 10.1(d), individuals who "knowingly furnish the NCAA or the individual's institution false or misleading information concerning the individual's involvement in or knowledge of matters relevant to a possible violation of an NCAA regulation" are guilty of unethical conduct. Groth was not only averse to dealing with allegations of NCAA violations in her department, it was undeniable that she covered them up, and in doing so, violated basic NCAA principles of ethical conduct.

Groth's handling of reports of Title IX violations will be detailed in the following chapter, and those results did not prove to be any better for her.

*   *   *

Groth was asked under oath about the August 22, 2007, 2.5-year contract that she had offered me just six days before I left the university:

Q   Had the 2.5-year contract offer been extended to her?
A   No. There's never been – I've never had a discussion with Terri on a multi-year contract.

But she was contradicted by General Counsel Mary Dugan who had written to my attorney Marc on September 5, 2007, just one week after I left the university:

[Patraw] refused the contract offer that was made to her on August 22, 2007, in a meeting with A.D. Groth.

Not only did Dugan admit that I was offered the contract, she pinpointed the date and location quite accurately. It gets even better. I had stayed in touch over the years with the former Senior Associate AD at ASU who had hired me there. He crossed paths with Groth at a conference about one month after I left the University of Nevada. He sent me an email on October 1, 2007:

> I spoke to Groth last week. She stated she offered you a contract and you turned it down.

UNR Provost Janet Vreeland testified:

A   Well, they made her an offer.
Q   And do you know if she accepted or rejected this offer?
A   I believe I was told she rejected.

Assistant Vice President of Human Resources Gena Jones testified:

Q   I believe you testified that Cary made an offer – a contract offer to Patraw? Yes.
A   My testimony is that Cary did discuss with me that she intended to make an offer. She wanted to – to look at her salary. And then I believe, in the conversation, it was clear to me that she – she had done that.

Associate AD John Nunn testified that Groth told him that she had offered me a new contract. My supervisor Cindy Fox even said that the 2.5-year contract was presented to me. I also had the contract offer in my possession. But, defying belief, Groth still testified that "there's never been – I've never had a discussion with Terri on a multi-year contract." Groth knew that this contract offer was an insurmountable obstacle for their defense. Although the final contract presented to me was clearly retaliatory – for fewer years and a smaller pay increase than originally discussed and included no university car for my use – it was nonetheless a multi-year offer. And based on that offer how could Groth tell a jury she had cause to end my employment when it was made just six days earlier? They had no case. She knew it; so she lied.

After years of supporting this lie by Groth, despite the overwhelming evidence proving its falsity, Dugan and her team of lawyers admitted to the Nevada Supreme Court in 2011 that Groth "offered her another appointment for 2.5 years with a raise, which Patraw rejected."

*   *   *

As previously detailed, I received "commendable" personnel evaluations throughout my entire tenure. Recognizing that these evaluations – which were signed by Executive Associate AD Cindy Fox, AD Cary Groth, and the university President – were problematic for their defense, UNR tried unsuccessfully to falsify my 2005 evaluation.

So now what? They needed something, anything.

Cindy Fox testified that on August 27, 2007, Groth held a meeting with her senior management team – Keith Hackett, John Nunn, Rory Hickok, and Cindy – to discuss my employment status. Cindy said that every one of them supported Groth's decision. However, Keith Hackett testified that he was not consulted about it. Keith said that I "had done a great job and was a good coach" and that "the Athletic Director had the same opinion." Keith had also articulated his support for me in an email:

> Terri . . . You have done a fantastic job of bringing the program so far. It has been a real pleasure to see what you have done . . . .

John Nunn testified that he was not asked for his input either. John said that Groth informed him that I had resigned. Rory Hickok had a sudden case of amnesia throughout his deposition. During his testimony, one of my attorneys scribbled me a note articulating his frustration with the number of "I cannot recalls" that Rory uttered. So I scribbled a note back and told him to ask Rory if he was a golfing and drinking buddy of Golf Coach Rich Merritt. Rory responded that he was both. With that, we had gotten all that we needed. Rory was an admitted friend of Merritt's, which would have made him easy to discredit in front of a jury. It was clear that Cindy had lied about her colleagues' consensus on Groth's retaliatory decision. What was even more appalling about Cindy's false testimony was that Cindy herself had attempted to stop Groth from retaliating against me. Despite being ordered by Groth to stay out of that final meeting between Groth, HR's Gena Jones, and me,

Cindy abruptly entered the room and tried to convince Groth that what she was doing was wrong.

Cindy was my friend and mentor and someone I had tremendous respect for when we worked together. Watching her actions in this case was one of the most difficult parts of the entire ordeal. In addition to her false testimony and her involvement in the fabricated personnel files, Cindy had to admit under questioning that she gave a check and offered basketball tickets to a witness while she and the witness were waiting to testify. Cindy had also called this witness at home and encouraged her to stay silent. She was also involved in the solicitation of student-athletes to send in false complaints about me, the absolute lowest action of all. It was a treacherous act against me as well as against the students who she was trying to use for her own end.

*   *   *

The university's case was falling apart all around them, deteriorating further with each deposition that took place. Since Groth had "looked in my personnel file and had nothing to use against me", the defendants fabricated another allegation about me. They accused me of sending anonymous emails to a colleague back in 2006. My attorney noted for the record that neither of my 2006 or 2007 personnel evaluations mentioned any allegations of sending anonymous emails. He then asked Groth, if this accusation were true, why hadn't she allowed me to meet with Steve Zink, Vice-President for Information Technology, the individual who had allegedly accused me. Groth responded that Zink "did not want to have a conversation with me." Zink was then called in and asked why he didn't want to meet with me. He testified that "Groth never told him that I wanted to meet with him." Clearly Dugan hadn't "worked with" this witness enough. This false allegation was dead on arrival. The defense team threw this allegation out there at the initial reinstatement hearing, but after Zink and Groth's contradictory testimony, they never brought it up again.

Hold that thought on anonymous emails. We will be touching on that again in a whole other manner . . .

*   *   *

If you have followed my case, you have heard over and over again from Groth and the university lawyers that I had resigned. During my final meeting with Groth on August 28, 2007, I asked her what she was going to tell the media. She said, "the only thing I will tell them is – if they ask me if you resigned I will tell them no. That is all I will say." That same evening she was inundated with calls from the media. Obviously unprepared and with no legal rationale for her decision, she told them that I had resigned! She could not keep her story straight on that very day. Her word wasn't even good for twenty-four hours. Because it was all over the press that I had resigned, and we had copies of the articles, Groth continued to tell anybody who would listen that I had resigned. However, much later Cindy was forced to admit that I had never submitted a resignation.

All of these lies bring me back to an account that I shared with you at the beginning of this book. Before I had ever met Groth, a colleague had shared the story of the important donor inappropriately confronting Groth about her personal life at a university gathering. And in response, Groth lied then too. Looking back on that story now, it was a harbinger of things to come. As Groth repeatedly lied about every material fact in my case, I found myself revisiting that story often. It was clear that lying and deception was the strategy she mastered to protect her career, and it was the same one that she deployed to damage the career of an honest and successful coach.

The NCAA articulates its "Standards of Ethical Conduct" under Bylaw 10.01.1:

> Individuals employed by or associated with member institutions to administer, conduct or coach intercollegiate athletics and all participating student-athletes shall act with honesty and sportsmanship at all times so that intercollegiate athletics as a whole, their institutions and they, as individuals shall represent the honor and dignity of fair play and the generally recognized high standards associated with wholesome competitive sports.

The NCAA goes further in "Exemplary Conduct" under Bylaw 19.01.2:

> Individuals employed by or associated with member institutions for the administration, the conduct or the coaching of intercollegiate athletics are, in the final analysis, teachers of young people. Their responsibility is an affirmative one, and they must do more than avoid improper conduct or questionable acts. Their own moral values must be so certain and positive that those younger and more pliable will be influenced by a fine example. Much more is expected of them than of the less critically placed citizen.

In what was merely a façade, Groth had admonished Golf Coach Merritt in his suspension letter for providing false and misleading information to the Director of Compliance, even threatening him with termination if he lied again:

> *. . . your having provided false or misleading information concerning each of the preceding violations, the last violation is particularly disappointing . . .* Should you provide false or misleading information or violate department or university policies again, you will be subject to immediate termination.

The Vision Statement for Nevada athletics is inscribed on its front door: "As an integral part of the university, the team will operate with the highest degree of integrity, fairness and accountability." But upon opening the door, one entered a department immersed in a culture of retaliation and betrayal. Cary Groth had no cause for ending my tenure at Nevada and she had no cause for sabotaging the 2007 season for the student-athletes in the soccer program. When it came time to look out for the student-athletes best interests, Groth sacrificed them. This was an abdication of her first and foremost responsibility as an athletic director – to care for the student-athletes under her leadership.

Looking back at all the lying and deceit and perjury and witness tampering, the burning question is why? The path of least resistance would have been to follow up on the relative minor complaints I had and taken care of them in the appropriate manner and within the confines of the university. Any competent and able manager or leader would have done nothing less. One lie or act of deception was followed by ten more to cover it up. It's often not the crime but the cover-up. Through her repeated and ongoing acts of retaliation, Groth catapulted herself into literally years of litigation that she could have avoided with simple honesty and by just doing her job.

I could not characterize the abyss that Groth et al. found themselves in more profoundly than Sir Walter Scott when he wrote, "Oh what a tangled web we weave, when first we practice to deceive."

CHAPTER 11

Direct Admissions of Retaliation

"Revenge is always the weak pleasure of a little and narrow mind."

~ Juvenal

By now you know that I had an exceptionally strong case. To be candid, my positive personnel evaluations alone would likely have been enough for a jury to see that Groth retaliated against me. But we had so much more, including several false statements under oath by Groth. The university's main witness had no credibility and my legal team would have a field day with her on the witness stand.

To add to the defense team's nightmare, we also obtained direct admissions that Groth retaliated against me. Under the law, when a plaintiff produces a direct admission of retaliation by the defendant – absent a settlement – the case must go to trial to be heard by a jury. "Direct evidence of animus [by the employer] . . . creates a triable issue . . . 'even if the evidence is not substantial.'" *Dominguez-Curry v. Nevada Transp. Dept.,* 424 F.3d 1027 (9th Cir. 2005). Any lawyer will vouch that it is a very rare thing to secure an admission of retaliation by the opposing party. In my case, we were fortunate enough to obtain three such admissions. The first was the stunning admission that occurred before witnesses in my final meeting with Groth:

"Terri you're a great, great coach. Nobody can deny that. I just need to move on. I looked in your personnel file. There was nothing to use against you."

"This has whistleblower retaliation written all over it," I responded.

"I know," replied Groth.

Although we needed no more than this one example of retaliation to meet minimum legal requirements to automatically propel my case on to a jury trial, we inexplicably got more.

On August 7, 2007, 21 days before my final day at Nevada, I had addressed the issue of my student-athletes being locked out of their locker room for football camp in a memorandum to Associate AD's Cindy Fox and Keith Hackett. In the memo, I concluded with the following statement:

> I highly recommend that Mr. Norcross be given a long lesson on the consequences of gender inequity in higher education. His lack of respect for the female student-athletes and staff at Nevada has the makings of a very expensive proposition for this university.

Groth gave us the second direct admission in her deposition:

Q Why did you terminate Terri?
A . . . If we didn't talk to the – if we didn't handle the facility situations, she would threaten that it would cost millions of – or a lot of money.

Groth's testimony is a direct admission that she retaliated against me because of my August 7, 2007, memorandum, which reported inequitable facility treatment for my female student athletes and the potential financial consequences of such discrimination to the university. She outright admitted that she retaliated against me for reporting Title IX violations in her department. That this admission came from a woman made it acutely more shameful.

It is axiomatic that a coach cannot bring a claim on behalf of his/her students, who were the victims of the discrimination. Only the victims have standing to seek relief. My memo was protecting the institution and its administration from potential liability. My statement was in no way a threat, as I had nothing to gain by it; it was a recommendation to take the necessary steps and precautions to avoid being in violation of important federal law. Groth knew this . . . or at least she should have since she was a member of the Secretary of Education's Commission on Opportunity in Athletics, which was created to review Title IX regulations and strengthen their enforcement. Groth also promoted herself as a Title IX expert witness in the UC Davis Title IX case that concluded in 2012. I was looking out for the best interests of the institution and the athletic director. I should have been praised for my diligence, not retaliated against. On that day in August 2007 when I wrote that note, we were all on the same side – at least as far as I knew we were.

As stated previously, I only needed one admission of retaliation for my case to automatically go before a jury of my peers. But as my case moved along, university officials continued to put their collective foot in their collective mouth. In NSHE and Groth's "Motion for Partial Summary Judgment" we received our third direct admission of retaliation. A summary judgment motion is a legal brief asking the court to throw out certain claims before the case goes to a jury trial. In the brief, Dugan's team of lawyers wrote on Page 7, line 11-12: "*She was not paid more because she complained or allegedly spoke freely about Title IX and NCAA infractions.*" This was a direct admission to the district court that they retaliated against me by punishing me financially! Remember that 5-year contract offer that suddenly became 2.5 years, the same offer that came up $10,000 short and minus the previously promised car?

Three strikes you're out? The game should have been over, right?

Absent an out-of-court settlement, there was no way that my case would not be heard before a jury. It was the law. It was my right. I had insurmountable evidence of three instances of retaliatory actions committed against me by the defense. My case was a slam-dunk. We knew it. UNR knew it. The judge knew it.

The defense would need help from on high to keep its losing case from going to trial.

CHAPTER 12

Big Mouse Traps

"When you have no basis for an argument, abuse the plaintiff."

~ Marcus Tullius Cicero

On May 22, 2008, Cindy Fox sent a letter across campus to the affirmative action office addressing issues in my case. The letter was cc'd to Harvey Whittemore, a longtime Nevada lobbyist, powerbroker, and a significant donor to the University of Nevada and its athletic department. There could be no plausible explanation as to why he was being copied on internal university communications, especially when he was not involved in my case in any capacity. Jeff and I racked our brains for an honest explanation but we came up empty. Whittemore, a close personal friend of US Senator Harry Reid, had been known to make big contributions to some of the state's most politically connected candidates and judges. He was well known as an influence peddler in Nevada. The minute I saw his name on this letter, I instinctively knew that it didn't pass the smell test. While I had heard many character traits ascribed to Whittemore during my tenure at Nevada, honest and ethical had not been among them.

On June 7, 2012, a Federal Grand Jury indicted Whittemore on four felony charges for making illegal campaign contributions to Senator Harry Reid and lying to federal officials, including the Federal Election Commission and the FBI. While I had no sympathy for Whittemore's plight, recalling that he had somehow been involved in my case gave me a decidedly eerie feeling. The indictment alleged that on a single day in 2007, Whittemore contributed $138,000 to Harry Reid's election campaign, using his family members and employees as illegal conduits. Under federal law in 2007, the maximum an individual could contribute to a candidate's entire campaign was $4,600. On May 30, 2013, Whittemore was convicted on three of the four felony charges after a jury trial in federal court. He faces up to 15 years in prison and $750,000 in fines. Whittemore joined the list of unscrupulous locals involved with the university and my case. Harry Reid has earmarked millions of dollars in federal funds for the University of Nevada, Reno, over the years. A campus building was named in his honor – the Harry Reid Engineering Laboratory. Both Reid and Whittemore had vested interest in the university. Remember, it was Harry Reid's son, Leif, who falsified court documents and filed for the illegal subpoena despite having no standing in my case.

In 2012, Whittemore was also involved in civil litigation with his former business partners. The accusations detailed in the multiple lawsuits included embezzlement, racketeering, and threats of murder and physical violence. This stuff does not just happen in the movies. Welcome to Reno, Nevada. Whittemore's business partners accused him of embezzling tens of millions of dollars from their company. This begs the question . . . how much of this allegedly dirty money ended up in university coffers?

I'll never know with any certainty why Whittemore had been included on the distribution list of an internal university letter about my case that was authored by Nevada Associate AD Cindy Fox. But considering his resume, I do know with *complete* certainty that it could not have been done for the cause of justice.

*   *   *

Post-employment retaliation began when University President Milton Glick sent UNR police officers outside their jurisdiction to my home to harass me on two separate occasions. One night I awoke to banging on my door and flashlights being shined in my windows. This was my first taste of what the real role of the UNRPD was. It was not an organization to enforce the law; rather it was an intimidation tool used to protect the university's public corruption operation.

Things only escalated after that. A colleague notified me that she had discovered that porn websites on the Internet had been created in my name. These sites were immediately shut down after I contacted the website's hosting company. There was only one logical suspect or suspects who could have been behind these indiscriminate and despicable acts to smear me publicly and personally.

Another individual who lived out of state but had first-hand experience with the corruption in the Nevada System of Higher Education had received a computer virus through her Facebook account. After taking her computer in to the Geek Squad for cleaning, it was discovered that the virus was sent with my name written within the code. Knowing that it did not come from me, a person she had never met, she reached out and notified me immediately. It was a veiled warning for her not to communicate with me, clearly from someone with much to hide. I've often wondered how many similar acts of sabotage had been committed against me that I never learned about. The conspiratorial nature of the retaliation war waged against me never ceased to amaze.

Knowing her career was on borrowed time, Groth sent an email to her entire staff ordering them to notify her if they saw me around town. Through discovery, the university was forced to produce a listing of all such reports that she had received. It was eerie, even frightening, to realize that my movements were being monitored by my former employer. The listing included such mundane entries as where and when I filled up my Jeep at the gas station, who I met for lunch, and who was in my car. No matter how trivial or innocuous these sightings of me living my life were, they apparently were deemed worthy of documenting. Unfortunately for them, it was a total waste of time. They were unable to catch me doing anything that would help their cause. Needless to say, in small town Reno I ran across some of my former colleagues on a regular basis. When I reviewed Groth's surveillance records of my daily movements, I immediately noticed that a number of these encounters were absent from the list. It was heartening to know that many of Groth's subordinates were disobeying her childish and desperate orders. She didn't have their respect and didn't deserve it.

A local blogger named Ryan Jerz – based on his user name, he preferred being called Mr. Jerz – was a self-described Nevada Wolf Pack fanatic, living his life vicariously through the football and basketball players at the school. He started attacking me on his blog apparently because he didn't want to believe that his beloved alma mater could be guilty of the deplorable actions that I had alleged. His wife also worked in the university alumni relations' office. To this day I have never met Mr. Jerz, although he inferred on his blog that we had. He also made claims about his knowledge of my case even though he had never worked with me, met me, or stepped foot in the courtroom. I was able to have his website shut down twice, which sent him scrambling to other hosting services. Groth, apparently impressed that she had a blogger in the community who was attacking me, even though she knew he peddled nothing but lies, created a new position in the athletic department and hired him! Groth's inexplicable employment of this blogger was just another example of the abuse of public trust by the UNR administration. Under Groth's leadership, the athletic department operated in the red almost every year. Despite the fact that she could have used the taxpayer money that she was entrusted with as a department head in scores of more appropriate and proactive ways, she squandered a portion of it to hire a man for her own nefarious purposes. Groth wanted Mr. Jerz under her thumb so she could exploit the fanatic local whose only claim to fame was harassing me online and publically defaming me with baseless accusations. Mr. Jerz's alliance with Groth ultimately caught up with both of them. More on that later.

*   *   *

I always knew the university did not have a defense or a case against me. I knew it because I had lived it. If there was ever a time to laugh during this journey, it was when General Counsel Mary Dugan's office produced a list of witnesses that they were planning to call to testify at my upcoming trial. Dugan asserted that each of these witnesses was going to testify about my character. I reviewed the list and did not recognize many of the names. Hmm, I wondered, how are these people going to testify to my character if they haven't as much as even met me? As I sifted through the names, I did a little research and made a few phone calls to learn exactly who these people were. It turned out that many of them were former Nevada soccer players from the era before I had arrived there. Someone in Dugan's office had failed to check and see which of these players had actually played for me. Again their venom was only outdone by their hapless incompetence. Not only was Dugan desperate, she was sloppy. The lengthy list was designed to intimidate me, and perhaps there was hope within Team Dugan that at least one name on the list would strike fear in my heart. Instead, the list only revealed the chaos that existed in the General Counsel's office on the eve of trial and confirmed that their case was baseless. I would later learn that most of the individuals on this list had never spoken to the university about my case nor had they been subpoenaed to appear at trial. The entire act of futility had been nothing more than a blatant act of intimidation.

*   *   *

The university had no case and they knew it and their liability was growing by the day. Doing the right thing was not in their lexicon. As my case slowly inched its way through the court system, some of my friends became concerned for my safety. The fact that the UNR Police Chief Adam Garcia had twice sent armed officers to harass me at my home coupled with the escalating acts of retaliation by Dugan, Groth, and others, it was clear that they would do anything to get me to drop my case. Two male friends, independently of one another, offered to help me secure a gun and teach me how to use it. They both strongly felt that I needed to be able to protect myself. Their concerns were later elevated when I received two separate electronic communications while my case was pending. On July 15, 2011 at 7:22 PM, I received a message stating: "You keep this up and someone is going to come after you!!! So just move on!!!!" On October 16, 2011 at 8:11 PM, I received a similar message which stated: "Move on or pay the ultimate price!!!!" The second message was identified as having been sent from Reno, NV on Charter Communications under the IP address 71.80.223.188. Before I left the university I was a Division I soccer coach at the top of my game. I arguably had the best team on campus. Now I was considering purchasing a gun to defend myself! What in the hell happened?! It was my life but I hardly recognized it.

*   *   *

Groth suspended, but did not fire, two coaches; one for having an inappropriate relationship with a student-athlete and the other – the golf coach – for repeatedly lying to the administration, assaulting a student-athlete, and violating NCAA rules.

Several Nevada coaches had received letters of admonishment for violating NCAA rules during Groth's tenure. In addition to the golf coach, another coach had four letters in her file, while three other coaches had two each. These coaches were all retained.

Groth, in a deposition, admitted that a coach was suspended from team travel for having a relationship with a student-athlete. The coach was allowed to continue coaching her team at practice and home competitions. Groth also acknowledged that an administrator was forced to travel with another Nevada team due to concerns with the head coach's behavior on the road around the student-athletes. Groth retained another head coach despite his DUI arrest and conviction; the coach in question was caught speeding through downtown Reno after leaving a strip club. When a female team demanded a meeting with the administration they levied charges of NCAA violations, retaliation, and sexual harassment against their head coach. Groth retained him.

Head Basketball Coach Mark Fox – my supervisor's husband – was publicly reprimanded by the conference office after nearly being arrested for stalking and threatening an official at an away contest. He apparently found losing a game unbearable and cause for physical violence. A police report was filed on Fox, and witnesses in attendance said he was very fortunate not to have been arrested. Prior to the intervention of the conference commissioner, the police officer had intended to take him into custody. Groth publicly defended Mark's behavior after the embarrassing incident made national news.

Mark Fox had a history of violence and unprofessional behavior at Nevada, including anger management issues that led to the destruction of university property. Both students and employees complained about Mark, but he was emboldened by Groth's failure to rein him in. Based on records we were able to obtain, we learned that, in addition to covering up the allegations of NCAA violations in his program, Groth also violated nepotism policies in her handling of complaints against him. In one example, Groth had received a complaint about Mark Fox via email that included a request for confidentiality. Rather than address the issues in the complaint, later the same day, Groth forwarded the email to Cindy, Mark's wife.

It seemed that the more baggage one carried under Groth, the safer his or her job was. Under the law, disparate treatment of employees is evidence of retaliation. The university lawyers knew that Groth's retention of these coaches – and their problematic personnel files – would be presented to the jury at trial. They also knew that it would be devastating to their defense.

*   *   *

In 2009, President Glick proposed a three-year contract extension for Groth to the NSHE Board of Regents with full knowledge that 1) my administrative reinstatement case had been remanded due to perjury, falsification of documents, and concealment of evidence by Groth et al.; 2) Groth had been implicated in criminal activity; and 3) the university was being investigated by the NCAA due to allegations of major violations in Groth's department. The chancellor and the regents, who were also fully in the loop regarding these discretions, rubber-stamped Groth's extension. The leadership of the entire system displayed no concern for the quality of the athletic program or the integrity of its athletic director.

An anonymous blog posted online in one of the Las Vegas newspapers was telling: "Unfortunately, corruption in higher education in Nevada is like mice in your house. When you see one, you really have 20. My suggestion: Buy the really big blue trap to make sure those you catch don't get away."

*   *   *

One day I was walking through a quiet hallway in the courthouse when a court bailiff pulled me aside. He told me he had been following my case and had been present at some of the hearings. He said that he really hoped that I would get justice, calling UNR's behavior in the courtroom a disgrace. If the bailiff could see right from wrong, so could the judge, and so could the local reporter.

And so could a jury of my peers once one was empanelled and allowed to hear the truth.

CHAPTER 13

Hometown Justice

"I have always thought, from my earliest youth till now that the greatest scourge an angry Heaven ever inflicted upon an ungrateful and sinning people, was an ignorant, a corrupt, or a dependent judiciary."

~ John Marshall

In 2012, Ty Robben, a Nevada citizen, led lawful and peaceful protests against corruption in Nevada's Attorney General's Office and judiciary. After several high profile demonstrations – with the "World's Largest Crime Scene Banner" at 4 ft tall x 150 ft long on display – in front of the AG's Office and the courthouse spurred significant media coverage, he was arrested on a trumped up misdemeanor assault charge. He spent a total of 22 days in jail – eight in solitary confinement – and nearly another month under house arrest with an ankle monitor. The judge who signed the arrest warrant was Judge John Tatro, the same judge who Ty had attempted to disqualify from his civil case due to judicial bias. The assault charge was eventually dropped.

In December 2012, Judge Tatro woke up to the sound of gunfire at his home around 4:30 am. Two shots entered the front door, passed through the living room, and exited through a sliding glass door. Ty Robben was questioned and immediately cleared. There has been no reported arrest to date but the police reviewed the judge's court calendar in search of suspects. This incident followed the highly publicized June 2006 shooting of Judge Chuck Weller. Judge Weller was shot in the chest through the window of his third-floor courthouse office in Reno, Nevada, by a sniper in the parking garage across the street. The sniper, Darren Mack, had appeared before Judge Weller in Mack's divorce case. Both Judge Tatro and Judge Weller had less than stellar reputations for rendering honest decisions in cases that came before them.

* * *

In previous chapters I've cited some examples of the questionable actions of judicial officers I encountered and hinted at the impropriety of other judges and of the entire judicial system in which they function. It would be beneficial for you, the reader, to have an in-depth overview of the State of Nevada judicial system – aside from my specific case. It will provide the proper backdrop for what I was up against in my encounter with Nevada justice and will bring the blatant incompetence and corruption of the judges and courts in Nevada into proper perspective. The Ty Robben's story is stunning, disturbing, and incomprehensible. It is also demonstrative of the lawlessness that exists in the state of Nevada, where the most fundamental constitutional rights are not recognized. In preparing for this and the next chapter, I have referenced the reports of reputable news reporters and the reports of legal experts and opinion makers all of which have been made public through the print and online media. The documented behavior of several Nevada judges during the course of their careers is relevant when assessing the Nevada judicial system as a whole. I was unfortunate enough to have my own personal experience with one of the judges highlighted in these reports.

* * *

In an extensive three-part series published in the *Los Angeles Times* in June 2006, entitled "JUICE VS. JUSTICE | A Times Investigation: In Las Vegas, They're Playing with a Stacked Judicial Deck," *Los Angeles Times* reporters Michael J. Goodman and William C. Rempel wrote in great detail about the questionable, even illegal, behavior of a number of Nevada judges. If the title wasn't enough to draw a picture for their readers, the reporters included this provocative statement as a subtitle:

Some judges routinely rule in cases involving friends, former clients and business associates – and in favor of lawyers who fill their campaign coffers.

Just think of the ramifications of that statement and weigh the chances for real justice in such a system.

When Judge Gene T. Porter ran for reelection, a group of Las Vegas lawyers sponsored a lavish fundraiser for him. The event was replete with "a sunset cruise on the Big Bear Queen . . . . [and] the evening blossomed into a festival of champagne, lobster and money" *(Goodman and Rempel)*. It was a brazen act even by Las Vegas standards. Robert D. Vannah, one of the attorneys involved in the event, had a case scheduled in Porter's court just a short four days following the fundraiser. One of the sponsors of the fundraiser summarized the sentiment of his lawyerly brethren:

> Giving money to a judge's campaign means you're less likely to get screwed. A $1,000 contribution isn't going to buy special treatment. It's just a hedge against bad things happening *(Goodman and Rempel)*.

The attorney for the defendant in the case had not contributed a dime to Porter's re-election. He feared that Porter would show bias and asked that Porter recuse himself due to the close proximity of the campaign gala to the trial. Porter refused claiming that he had no bias or prejudice. Porter also denied a request that the case be delayed. The case went to trial resulting in Porter's order that the defendant pay the plaintiff $1.5 million in damages.

Judge Porter also owed money to the principal of a law firm and ruled in the firm's favor in six separate cases. There was no documentation that Porter ever revealed his debt to the opposing sides.

The attorneys familiar with the way things go in Nevada call it "hometown justice." But the "justice" meted out by the judges in Nevada goes far beyond the spirit of that characterization. It is a "good-old-boy culture of cronyism and chumminess that accepted conflicts of interest as 'business as usual'" *(Goodman and Rempel)*. It was also described in the *Times* article as being just part of Nevada's culture of government-approved vice including "prostitution, gambling, drive-through marriages and quickie divorces." It was just the way it was and anyone operating within that culture had better get accustomed to it. John C. Kirkland, an attorney from Santa Monica, California, assessed his experience with the Nevada judicial system in the following succinct manner:

I don't think what goes on in Nevada bears any resemblance to a justice system. It's an old-boy network. It's not a legal system *(Goodman and Rempel)*.

The Nevada system of justice consists of state and federal judges who hear both civil and criminal cases. In their extensive report about Nevada judges, the *Times* reporters made the following observations:

These state judges often dispense a style of wide-open, frontier justice that veers out of control across ethical, if not legal, boundaries. The consequences reach beyond Nevada, affecting people in other states . . . . *(Goodman and Rempel)*.

We Americans are proud of our justice system and are taught from the time we are in elementary school to trust in it because it is fair and unbiased. It's what we have come to expect. But in the incestuous atmosphere in Nevada, the district court judges often rule in cases involving "friends, former clients, business associates, even in cases touching people to whom they owe money." Needless to say this cannot be an environment that fosters an impartial judicial system.

Judge James C. Mahan awarded over $4.8 million in judgments and fees in a dozen cases in which he had personal ties to those who received these monetary awards. District Judge Nancy Saitta, running unopposed, raised $120,000 in a single reelection campaign. All lawyers and law firms that had given $500 or more had cases pending before her *(Goodman and Rempel)*. Saitta ordered that more than $1 million be awarded to an accountant and his attorneys, two of whom had sponsored a fundraiser for her during the time when the case was still ongoing. District Judge Sally Loehrer also had apparent conflicts with campaign contributions from attorneys who presented cases in her court. Of the fifty-four attorneys who contributed $500 or more to her reelection, fifty-one had cases pending before her. On the evening before one of her fundraisers, four law firms went together and gifted her with "12 bottles of wine a 13-inch TV, two DVD players, a gas grill, dinner for four at Zefferino's restaurant, two theater tickets, two golf lessons and a pool float with two beach towels" *(Goodman and Rempel)*. All four law firms had cases scheduled for Loehrer's courtroom.

District Judge Joseph S. Pavlikowski, accepted a discounted wedding reception for his daughter from Frank "Lefty" Rosenthal, a member of the Chicago mob. Later, Pavlikowski ruled in Rosenthal's favor in three criminal cases about his fitness to run a casino. Ultimately, Pavlikowski was rewarded with a senior judgeship commissioned by the Nevada Supreme Court. Judge Donald M. Mosley gave thousands of dollars in campaign funds to his girlfriend in direct violation of the state Code of Judicial Conduct. That these judges were rarely called to task for their questionable behavior was more astonishing than the behavior itself. Many were promoted to even higher positions of trust. Dean Heller, Nevada's then-secretary of state and chief elections officer, explained the lack of oversight in this way:

> Heller said the Legislature gave him only seven people to monitor elections and the campaign reporting of up to 1,000 candidates statewide. Worse, he said, legislators "won't give us authority to audit or even look for reporting irregularities unless we receive a complaint in writing. We get a lot of complaints over the phone, but not many want to put it in writing" *(Goodman and Rempel)*.

Judge Jeffrey Sobel was removed from the bench as a result of his statement to an attorney that he was screwed in Sobel's court because the attorney hadn't contributed any campaign funds. Although the Nevada Commission on Judicial Discipline investigated Sobel, removed him from the bench and "permanently barred him from serving as an elected or appointed judicial officer in Nevada," *(Goodman and Rempel)* they did allow him to mediate and arbitrate cases which still gave him power over the outcome of cases. Mosely's defense about his caprice was that he thought the loan to his girlfriend was short-term. However, no loans – short or long term – were acceptable according to Canon 7 of the code that stated at the time that judicial candidates "should not use . . . campaign contributions for purposes unrelated to the campaign." After the Mosely incident the canon was strengthened and now falls under Canon 5: judicial candidates "shall not use or permit the use of campaign contributions for the private benefit of the candidate or others" *(Goodman and Rempel)*. Perhaps Mosely can take some pride in being partially responsible for the harsher restriction. His girlfriend testified that she thought it was a gift, which apparently it was since she admitted to having never paid him back. Whatever she chose to do with the money she owed her thanks to Mosley's campaign contributors.

Don Chairez, a former Nevada state judge, provided this honest assessment:

> Nevada judges find themselves losing or bargaining away their integrity or independence *(Goodman and Rempel)*.

The lawyers were, of course, all aware of the state of justice in Nevada. Veteran Las Vegas lawyer, Cal Potter III, told the reporters that "outside law firms just don't trust Nevada Courtrooms." Even the Nevada Supreme Court justices depend on collecting money for their own campaigns. The overt and blatant solicitation of funds from attorneys by judges and justices for their reelection goes against the grain, the ideal and what we have been taught to believe about blind justice. Although Nevada judicial canons state that judges must recuse themselves when there is a conflict of interest, no one seems to pay any attention to them.

The *Los Angeles Times* review of Judge Gene Porter's cases indicated that in sixty-one of them he had conflicts of interest and that in fifty of them no statement was forthcoming from Porter about the existence of such conflicts. Porter ordered that attorney Matthew Callister be appointed as a $200-an-hour caretaker of assets in a case before him. Callister and Porter had met in high school and had been life-long friends.

One could blame the culture of vice and "anything goes" for the fast and loose attitude that exists within the Nevada judicial system. But surely there's more to it than that. The requirement for the judges to raise campaign funds obviously places the judges in untenable positions. But, bottom line, perhaps it comes down to morals. A scrupulous judge with strength of character would surely fulfill his or her judicial responsibilities without bias regardless of campaign contributions received from an attorney. But a weaker individual, lacking in character and morals, would more easily succumb to the pressures of a quid pro quo environment. Apparently, there have been more of the latter than of the former in the

Nevada Judicial System. In one campaign, records indicate that sitting judges collectively raised $1.7 million in campaign donations, many of which were from lawyers and casinos that had pending cases before the district courts. Attorney Steve Morris, spoke of some lawyers being in "almost terror of not giving to judges seeking campaign contributions" *(Goodman and Rempel)*. A relatively small contribution of $500 to $1000 may not help an attorney win a case but it could get him on an early docket. Lawyers learned not to speak out against the system. "You pay dearly when you visit their courtroom." Some lawyers referred to bucking the system as the "kiss of death."

In 2002, attorney Grenville Pridham tried to break the tide of corruption by running for a judgeship and refusing to take any donations. He lost his election in a landslide. Still working as an attorney after his failed campaign, he couldn't help but notice that his cases would generally be called last regardless of when they were scheduled to be presented. Obviously contributions are not only desired, they are expected.

Juice vs. Justice? "This is a juice town", Las Vegas attorneys openly concede *(Goodman and Rempel)*.

CHAPTER 14

A Judge in Their Pocket
Chief Justice Nancy Saitta

"Take all the robes of all the good judges that have ever lived on the face of the earth, and they would not be large enough to cover the iniquity of one corrupt judge."
~ Henry Ward Beecher

Although the public information officer for the state courts in Las Vegas warned judges not to speak to *LA Times* reporters Goodman and Rempel, District Court Judge Nancy Saitta spoke up and told them she had nothing to hide. The *Times* focused on a case involving Medical Device Alliance Inc., a company that manufactured liposuction machines that landed in Judge Saitta's courtroom. The company was involved in a dispute between its minority shareholders and its founder and CEO, Donald McGhan. Judge Saitta was privately criticized by attorneys who felt that George C. Swarts, a CPA she appointed as a receiver – someone to manage the company while it was involved in the dispute – had inordinate power with the judge. It apparently wasn't just their imagination. Swarts reportedly boasted that he could do anything he wanted with regards to the case and that the "judge will do anything I ask" *(Goodman and Rempel)*. And what Swarts wanted more than anything was to drag the case out so that he could keep profiting from his receivership. CEO McGhan and a group of stockholders filed a complaint that Swarts was making bad decisions due to his lack of expertise in the business.

McGhan also tried to get Saitta disqualified from the case, declaring that Judge Saitta had made decisions unfavorable to McGhan on three separate occasions even though she hadn't been presented with any evidence or heard the testimony. McGhan's attorneys had responded aggressively by filing a motion, which stated the obvious:

> By passing judgment . . . without a trial, Judge Saitta can no longer be considered a fair and neutral arbiter . . . under the law, she is required to step aside (Goodman and Rempel).

Despite this, she remained on the case. But the opposition to Saitta did not die. She came under attack for refusing to allow anyone to have access to paperwork supporting claims for fees for Swarts and his lawyers. She was obviously shielding them from exposure. The paperwork being sought contained details for the $524,680 in fees that had been billed in a single year. McGhan's attorney called her refusal to either deny the fees or allow access to the supporting documents "a great injustice" (Goodman and Rempel).

Undaunted by the pressure and bad PR, Saitta approved the large fee and a second one for the following year that totaled another $662,411, as well as an additional 18 percent interest to be paid on outstanding fees and a request that Swarts' attorneys' fees be doubled. In the Times interview with Saitta she predictably had a case of amnesia, claiming not to be able to recall the specifics of this case since she heard over 2,400 cases a year.

Saitta received financial support in her newly announced campaign for re-election from one of Swarts' attorneys, J. Randall Jones, while the Medical Device Alliance case was still ongoing. Jones held a fundraiser for her with a suggested minimum contribution of $500. During the lead-up to the case, Saitta approved four motions presented by Swarts' attorneys. At the fundraiser, Saitta personally greeted those attending. Campaign records indicate that at least eighteen of the contributors were attorneys with cases pending before her at the same time. She nonchalantly described her participation at the fundraiser as meeting and shaking hands with people and "there [was] a bowl for the checks" (Goodman and Rempel). An estimated $20,000 was collected for Saitta at the fundraiser. She ran unopposed and was, of course, reelected. Swarts wasn't elected to anything but he didn't care. Over the course of his receivership his and his lawyers' fees ordained by Saitta topped $1 million.

*   *   *

Former Las Vegas City Councilman, Steve Miller, on January 9, 2012, in his blog, *Inside Vegas*, posted an article entitled, "Nevada Supreme Court Justice Nancy Saitta's mob associations may haunt her re-election bid." It tells the story of Scott David Fau who stopped by Rick Rizzolo's Crazy Horse Too topless bar on August 4, 1995. His body was found several hours later next to the railroad tracks behind the bar. Eyewitnesses claimed that Fau had been beaten to death by Crazy Horse Too bouncers.

Subsequently, Fau's widow filed a wrongful death suit against the nightclub and its owner, Rick Rizzolo. The case, which was eventually held in July 1997, was assigned to Nancy Saitta. On August 1, 1997, the *Las Vegas Sun* published a story entitled, "Topless club sued over patron's death." After this story ran, the City of Las Vegas shut the Crazy Horse Too down. The club was seized by the US Government and Rizzolo and fifteen Crazy Horse Too employees were arrested and later convicted of felonies.

Judge Saitta dismissed the Fau lawsuit two weeks before it was to be heard. After the Fau family attorney filed an appeal with the Nevada Supreme Court, Saitta reversed her decision and decided she would hear the case after all. Fau's attorney asked that the scope of testimony include a declaration filed by Pathologist Griffith Thomas, M.D. as to cause of death, evidence of other incidence of abusive treatment of patrons at the bar – including one which resulted in the quadriplegia of a man – prior felony records of the bouncers involved, photos of the decedent, as well as important eyewitness accounts. Witness Dan Kennedy's account of the actual beating coincided with pathologist Griffith Thomas' assessment of the cause of death. Kennedy stated under oath that the bouncers were kicking and beating Fau unmercifully even after he stopped moving. They were even stomping and jumping on Fau who was either dead or unconscious at the time.

Rather than immediately ruling on what could and could not be introduced into court, Saitta delayed the proceeding. After the trial resumed, Saitta refused to allow Kennedy's eyewitness testimony or Griffith's pathology report. Inexplicably, Saitta instructed the jury that they could not consider "blunt force trauma" as a cause of death – an odd omission for someone beaten to death. After what Miller characterized as a "mini-trial" and "restrictive jury instructions by the judge" the jury ruled in favor of Rizzolo leaving the family of the dead man devastated.

The Fau family attorney was led to Kennedy by James "Buffalo Jim" Barrier, the owner and operator of All State Auto and Marine and a commercial neighbor of the Crazy Horse Too. Prior to the trial, Rizzolo had filed defamation lawsuits against Steve Miller, Dan Kennedy, Jim Barrier and the weekly tabloid newspaper where Miller was employed. These lawsuits all "randomly" wound up on Saitta's docket while curiously Rizzolo's attorneys, Dean Patti and Tony Sgro, had been her chief campaign fundraisers. At one point, Saitta had five straight cases involving Rizzolo but refused to withdraw from any of them.

Miller was not spooked by the defamation lawsuits and continued to pursue the story of Rizzolo and Saitta. Miller refused to answer interrogatories from Rizzolo's attorneys and would not give a deposition for the defamation case. He claimed immunity based on Nevada's Reporter's Shield Law. Saitta was determined to bring Rizzolo's defamation lawsuits to trial despite the fact that Miller refused to cooperate. Undaunted, Miller continued writing articles and editorials about the impropriety of Saitta presiding over all lawsuits involving Rizzolo.

A Motion for Gag Order that Rizzolo filed against Miller to silence him surfaced, not surprisingly, in Saitta's court. Again, Miller refused to attend or mount a defense. Miller was relentless and continued his articles about Rizzolo and Saitta. Miller's reporting drew the attention of the Nevada press and the ACLU. On the day that Saitta had to rule on the gag order request, members of the press, counsel for the Donrey Media Group, which operates the *Las Vegas Review-Journal*, and attorneys from the ACLU were present in the courtroom. It was one of the few times that Saitta ruled against Rizzolo and denied his request for a gag order.

Miller continued writing articles questioning how one judge could "randomly" be assigned to cases involving the same litigant. Saitta blamed it on "coincidence." But Miller learned through an insider that "the court clerk allegedly would pull cases involving Rizzolo and place them aside until Saitta's name was next in rotation." And, later, according to Miller, "Saitta was observed attending a party at Rizzolo's Canyon Gate estate and hugging and kissing her host."

> The court system in Clark County is intended to provide a random selection process that fairly assigns judges to cases. This process was meant to guarantee that the same judge would not preside over multiple cases involving the same litigant *(Miller, 2012)*.

At the defamation hearing of Jim Barrier, Judge Saitta's opening statement was stunning:

> Mr. Rizzolo has a good name in the community *(Miller, 2012)*.

In July 2000, Barrier had been interviewed by a *Las Vegas Review Journal* reporter and infuriated Rizzolo by accusing him of being involved in racketeering and political corruption. Five years later, Rizzolo pleaded guilty to racketeering and was sentenced to serve time in a federal prison.

Ultimately Saitta removed herself from four of five cases involving Rizzolo but did so only after pressure from the media. However, she retained jurisdiction over the most important case – the Fau family wrongful death lawsuit against Rizzolo.

*   *   *

According to Miller, Saitta was quiet for a while but four years later she emerged in another controversial matter according to an article in the *Las Vegas Sun* entitled, "Judge Lands in Middle of Feud," by Sam Skolnik, published on July 21, 2006. Judge Elizabeth Gonzalez had found in favor of Barrier in a long-standing dispute with Rizzolo over parking spaces with neighboring strip clubs including the Crazy Horse Too. Not satisfied with Gonzalez's ruling, Rizzolo's attorneys took the matter up with Saitta who issued an order that was more favorable to Rizzolo although Saitta hadn't been the judge of record for years – it was one of Rizzolo's cases that she had recused herself from. The judge's clerk was instructed to stamp Saitta's approval on Rizzolo's request. According to Miller in an *Inside Vegas* article posted August 15, 2005, "A Judge in their Pocket", the judge of record, Judge Gonzalez referred to Barrier as the plaintiff. In Saitta's order, she referred to Barrier as the defendant.

Judge Gonzalez – who was the only judge with jurisdiction over the case – signed her order on September 23, 2004. Then, Judge Nancy M. Saitta signed her order – without jurisdiction – five days later on September 28 *(Miller, 2005)*.

Why did Saitta interfere in a case that another judge was presiding over? According to Miller, Rizzolo was one of her biggest campaign contributors. Published reports also revealed that Saitta's name surfaced in an FBI investigation into Rizzolo. Another convicted felon "told agents that Rizzolo claimed he had paid Saitta $40,000 to $50,000, in under-the-table, cash contributions" *(Skolnik)*.

*   *   *

In his paper for the *Northwestern Journal of Law & Social Policy, Winter 2008*, Bronson D. Bills explored the dangers of electing judges:

> Judicial elections require judges to solicit contributions from donors who will likely appear before them in court – a fact that may influence a judge's future decision making, and certainly, if nothing else, creates the appearance of judicial impropriety. Judicial elections also invite unqualified candidates with deep pockets to run for judgeships, destroy the traditional respect for the bench and virtually guarantee that judges will base their decisions partially, if not completely, upon the vicissitudes of popular politics instead of the law *(Bills, 1-2)*[1].

The paper cited the ouster of incumbent Chief Justice Nancy Becker in 2006 from the Nevada Supreme Court. In her bid for reelection for what was commonly referred to as Seat G on the court, she was "ousted by an arguably much less qualified opponent [Nancy Saitta] who, with the help of several wealthy special interest groups and the press grossly, carelessly, and shameless[ly] distorted the facts of *Guinn* to the voting public" *(Bills, 31)*. Becker's ouster was blamed in part on an unpopular

---

[1]   See original article for citations.

opinion she handed down with the majority on a civil tax matter in *Guinn v. Nevada State Legislature*. Becker was the first justice in the majority decision to run for reelection after *Guinn*.

Judges must not only be concerned about the cases before them but about reprisals resulting from unpopular decisions and rulings they make, especially since funds can easily be amassed to replace them in their bids for reelection. In his paper, Bills provided the following information about Seat G:

> . . . prior to the Seat G election, several Nevada judges, including then-Judge Nancy Saitta (the winner of the Seat G race), were the subject of a *Los Angeles Times* article that demonstrated that numerous judges, including Saitta, not only heard cases involving campaign donors (a conflict of interest?), but also issued rulings that were favorable to the various campaign donors (another conflict of interest?) (*Bills, 30*)[2].

> Judge Saitta's qualifications . . . were less than impressive. She was the most reversed District Court Judge in Nevada and an extremely inefficient lower court judge, who had not published a single opinion or academic article . . . . Moreover, not only was Saitta unqualified for the Supreme Court, but she was also tied to several wealthy special interest groups who sought to oust Justice Becker. Additionally, she had, in the past, presided over and ruled in favor of several controversial cases involving campaign contributors (*Bills, 50*)[3].

As it turned out, the issue came down to Becker being part of the majority in the unpopular *Guinn* decision. Qualifications obviously didn't matter, which Saitta was well aware of since she focused her advertising not on what she could bring to the court but rather on the *Guinn* decision.

Chief Justice Becker's ouster was the first time in American history that a sitting state supreme court justice had been voted out based on a single opinion in a civil decision – a decision that was legally justifiable

[2]   Ibid.

[3]   Ibid.

although politically unpopular. The fact that she was replaced by a less qualified individual is an example of the dangers of judicial elections. Such a result jeopardizes the entire judicial system in a state court and tips the scales of justice to the powerful and wealthy:

> Saitta had the powerful backing of various wealthy special interest groups who sought to oust Justice Becker. Indeed, it is well known that Saitta was approached by certain powerful and wealthy attorneys in Nevada who wanted to remove Becker because she had issued decisions that were contrary to a variety of the interests they frequently represented. In this election, it was Saitta's capacity to use wealthy special interest groups – an ability unrelated to judicial skill – that allowed her to win the race, not her qualifications *(Bills, 26)*[4].

*   *   *

In a column appearing in the *Las Vegas Review Journal* on November 12, 2007, Jane Ann Morrison noted that Saitta had been forced to confess that she had inflated her academic credentials. Saitta claimed on her 2006 campaign website that she had been an associate professor at the University of Nevada, Las Vegas, when in actuality, she had been a part-time instructor who taught just one class. "When her resume is stripped of falsehoods, there is nothing left but her robe," one lawyer said *(Maimon)*. It is worth noting that UNLV is a division of the Nevada System of Higher Education, a named defendant in my case.

*   *   *

The *Las Vegas Review Journal* reported the results of its "Judicial Performance Evaluation" in a biennial series called "Judging the Judges," in which lawyers anonymously rate the judges and justices that they practice in front of. Each jurist is rated on categories such as judicial competence, freedom from bias and impropriety, case preparation, and professional courtesy. Supreme Court Justice Saitta has routinely found herself at the bottom of the judicial retention scores – the percentage of lawyers who recommended that the judge or justice be retained.

---

[4]   Ibid.

A common perception among out-of-state lawyers speaking with the *LA Times* about their experiences in Nevada is that justice "is just another form of legalized gambling." Unsurprisingly, the American Tort Reform Foundation has repeatedly placed Nevada on its list of "judicial hellholes."

You will note that the name of Judge and Justice Nancy Saitta appeared quite often in the articles about judicial malfeasance. I was unfortunate enough to encounter her during my journey to find justice. She was named the Chief Justice of the Nevada Supreme Court in September 2011, one month before my case would be heard.

With liberty and justice for . . . .

CHAPTER 15

Deposing a Judge

"Power does not corrupt. Fear corrupts . . . perhaps the fear of a loss of power."

~ John Steinbeck

It was May 2009, just days before my May 11th trial date, when I learned first-hand that the Nevada judicial system was really not a justice system at all. We had just finished *four days* of oral arguments – which any lawyer will confirm is *well* outside the norm – in front of the *third* judge assigned to my case. There was clearly nothing ordinary about the handling of my case by the Nevada judiciary.

Even though Nevada state law dictates that a judge must declare any potential conflicts he has with all parties to the proceeding, most of the judges we encountered chose not to follow that dictum. In the Nevada judicial system, a case is 'randomly' assigned to a judge. It is then the judge's responsibility to review the case and become acquainted with the parties on both sides in order to discover if he or she has any conflicts of interest. If so, the judge must recuse himself or seek a waiver from the parties to remain on the case. If there are no conflicts, they can accept the case. At any rate, in an ideal world, that's the way it's supposed to go.

But as I learned in the Nevada judicial system's school of hard knocks, the laws were seldom adhered to by those who were elected to uphold them.

My case was first assigned to Judge Steve Elliott. He accepted it and did not come forth with any statement of conflict or intention to withdraw. I soon realized that Elliott's wife, Mendy Elliott, sat on the Board of Directors of the Athletic Association of University of Nevada (AAUN), which is the central fundraising arm of Wolf Pack athletics. It serves as the umbrella organization for all developmental efforts associated with University of Nevada athletics. As I write this, her photo is still on the Athletic Department website as a continuing member of the board.

Since my claims were against the university athletic department where Elliott's wife held a high profile position, it was painfully obvious that Judge Elliott had an undeniable conflict.

During Elliott's review of the case and parties involved, he became aware that Cary Groth was a principal in the matter. He was also undoubtedly aware that his wife, Mendy, had received several gifts from Groth, including two sets of custom golf clubs. And Mendy Elliott, along with her husband, the judge, was a significant supporter of and donor to the athletic department. Her husband's acceptance of the case was demonstrative of the blatant and deep-seated disregard that the district court judges had for the Nevada Code of Judicial Conduct, which states:

. . . a judge is disqualified whenever the judge's impartiality might reasonably be questioned.

Jeff and I were more than reasonable in questioning his impartiality.

Under Nevada Rules of Practice, each party is allowed one peremptory challenge to the assignment of a judge and has the right to dismiss a judge without stating a reason. We exercised this option and removed Elliott from the case. The case was then assigned to Connie Steinheimer. Steinheimer presided over it for 13 months when she suddenly and curiously transferred it to Judge Patrick Flanagan less than four months before trial. No reason was given other than Chief Judge Steinheimer had made an administrative decision to transfer it.

* * *

On May 5, 2009, Judge Flanagan – just seven hours after inexplicably denying our motion for sanctions against the university lawyers and Leif

Reid for the ASU fraud – issued an order dismissing my entire case on a procedure called summary judgment. It was unconscionable! I had 19 claims against the university, among them retaliation, defamation and breach of contract. Because the facts and law were undeniably on my side on *all* 19 claims, my expanded legal team (I will introduce them to you later) and I immediately knew the fix was in. The university had provided no authenticated evidence to support their defense and proved to be utterly incompetent in their briefing. Of course with the evidence and law so overwhelmingly against them, they might just as well have been writing about ice fishing in Alaska. Having read their briefs and watched them work, it was clear that Robison and Arrascada were not brought into the UNR defense team for their legal competence; they were brought in to sabotage my case by using their good-old-boy – I use that term gender neutrally – network in the judicial system. Remember that hole that UNR had dug – and kept digging – while looking around for someone to bail them out? They found that person in Judge Patrick Flanagan.

But twenty-four hours after the devastating news that my case was thrown out Jeff called me with some good news. The "Judge" in his hastiness to dismiss my case had failed to address five of the 19 claims. The university had made no effort to dismiss these five claims in their briefing, which explained why the judge never addressed them in his order of dismissal.

"You are going to trial on five claims" Jeff said, trying to lift my spirits.

Jeff immediately filed a notice to the judge, "Emergency Notice Seeking Confirmation of Trial Date on Remaining Claims." After this filing, there was nothing but silence from Dugan and her unscrupulous team of lawyers. The "Judge" also went silent. Trial was only days away. We waited for a response. And waited. The "Judge" was backed into a corner, his judicial fraud exposed. We got nothing.

The May 11th trial date quietly passed with no movement from the "Judge" or Team Dugan. The judge of record was AWOL from his own proceeding.

*　　*　　*

During these anxious few days after Judge Flanagan's abrupt and inexplicable dismissal of my case, the following blog was posted anonymously on a May 7, 2009, *Reno Gazette Journal* article:

This can really be a great book followed by a movie. Especially the part of the story when you find out that Judge Flanagan is a very close friend with UNR's Chief Counsel, Mary Dugan . . . he never should have sat in judgment of this case. Nevada needs a major makeover . . .

The blog was quickly removed from the RGJ, but not before a friend had contacted me about it and printed it off. I'll explain in a subsequent chapter how the *Reno Gazette Journal* did not function as an objective news organization; rather it served as the mouthpiece for the UNR administration. That being said, it was hardly surprising when the posting was quickly removed.

After Judge Flanagan's undisclosed personal relationship with Mary Dugan – the university official who engineered the retaliation campaign against me – was publicly exposed, it didn't take long to uncover that the judge had several conflicts of interest with other interested parties in my case.

So, on May 18, 2009, Jeff filed a motion to disqualify Judge Flanagan. The motion and its accompanying "affidavit of bias" laid out the specific allegations of bias that we had amassed against the judge. This affidavit contained evidence of Judge Flanagan's bias including the fact that he was a "very close friend" with the lead defense counsel, Mary Dugan; that he had a close personal relationship with Senator Harry Reid whose son, Leif, had an interest in this case; and, before assuming his judgeship, Flanagan had been Dugan's co-counsel while defending former UNR administrator, Craig Beattie, in another university retaliation case.

The close personal relationship that Flanagan had with Dugan had not been disclosed by the judge although the law demanded it. Surely that friendship had to come to mind when, in late April, he reviewed my case which included the fact that I had reported his friend Dugan's falsification of evidence to law enforcement. Judge Flanagan dismissed my case one week later.

Judge Flanagan is a quadriplegic and shares a common interest in stem cell research with Senator Harry Reid. On a campaign website for his reelection for judge, Flanagan was referred to as a prime candidate for stem cell research in the same article in which a photo was posted of Flanagan and Senator Reid smiling for the camera. Reid had publicly declared stem cell research one of his top priorities. The two of them even campaigned on the cause together. Leif Reid, the senator's son, was the attorney who had illegally sought a subpoena to secure the manufactured employment records from Arizona State University. Not surprisingly, Judge Flanagan ultimately denied this motion, despite the indisputable evidence that Leif Reid committed fraud upon the court. A judge who believed the words in the oath he took would put personal issues aside even if it meant sanctioning the son of a man who was trying to help him walk again. Flanagan found himself in a self-imposed dilemma that would have been avoided had he followed the law and removed himself from the case. It is important to note that Senator Reid has a deep involvement in the Nevada judicial system since it is he who nominates individuals for the much-coveted federal judgeships in Nevada.

In 2005-06, Flanagan was a private-practice attorney who was hired to defend UNR administrator Craig Beattie in another university retaliation case. Flanagan was therefore a member of UNR's legal team, working with General Counsel Dugan to defend Beattie and the university. The plaintiff in the case against Beattie was none other than Dr. Hussein. As Judge Flanagan reviewed the particulars of my case, he saw that Hussein was listed as a material witness who would testify at trial. Flanagan most assuredly recollected that he represented Beattie just three years earlier. In preparation for my upcoming trial, Flanagan was made aware that the scope of Hussein's testimony would include discussion of matters pertaining to the retaliation he endured at the hands of Flanagan's then-client Craig Beattie. Consider this argument between Jeff and UNR lawyers Robison and Hilsabeck at the April 28, 2009, hearing in my case just seven days before Judge Flanagan dismissed it:

ROBISON: . . . As the Court knows, the designation of Dr. Hussein as a witness in this case describes his involvement something like he has experience with UNR regarding whistleblower retaliation or actions.

JEFF: . . . the Court has an understanding of the substantial similarity we're claiming. He reports animal abuse . . . they commence a proceeding to terminate [him] within 30 days of that. And that results in six months of Chapter Six litigation that ends up with a hearing in front of Judge Fondi . . . where Judge Fondi finds and the unanimous hearing panel of faculty agrees . . . that there was no basis for the Chapter Six complaint and that it should be dismissed . . .

HILSABECK: . . . It simply is too inflammatory, it's too prejudicial . . . I believe that what happened in the Hussein case and those types of issues just shouldn't be allowed.

JEFF: . . . this evidence would come in through Dr. Hussein to talk about his protected activity of reporting animal abuse. And I'm not going to respond to the there was no animal abuse comment . . . If the Court wants to hear about the animal abuse, I can go on all day about it.

JUDGE FLANAGAN: No, that's all right.

JEFF: If Dr. Hussein is not allowed to testify, I don't see how I can get the animal abuse in . . .

Flanagan, while a practicing attorney, had represented Beattie at this Chapter Six hearing before Judge Michael Fondi. It is indisputable that Judge Flanagan had previously served as a lawyer on matters in contention and that he had knowledge of disputed evidentiary facts in my case – due to his prior representation of Dr. Beattie. At this April 28, 2009, hearing, Jeff argued that we should be permitted to present the Beattie evidence to the jury to show that the university was immersed in a culture of retaliation. UNR lawyers argued to keep this evidence out. Judge Flanagan – who was in the position to decide this important issue – had an inherent bias due to his involvement with Beattie. He dismissed my case seven days after the hearing, and, in doing so, ensured that his former client's actions were shielded from public exposure. According to the Nevada Code of Judicial Conduct, "A judge **shall** disqualify himself when he has personal knowledge of facts that are in dispute in the proceeding; and/or when he has served as a lawyer in the matter in controversy." Judge Flanagan's representation of Beattie is an established fact that had been conceded by UNR. The word "shall" in legal terms means must. There is no gray area. He was required by law to recuse himself from my case but failed to do so.

The decision in *Hoff v. Eighth Judicial District Court*, 378 P.2d 977 Nev. (1963) said it most succinctly:

> The actions of a district judge, disqualified by statute, are not voidable merely, but void.

*   *   *

As soon as he was served with the motion to disqualify, Judge Flanagan – under the law – was prohibited from handing down further orders or decisions in my case. The jurisdiction of my case was at least temporarily wrested from him. He was then forced to do one of two things. For one, he could have filed an affidavit under the penalty of perjury affirming or denying our bias allegations. His second option was to immediately recuse himself from my case. He did neither. Instead, he chose to ignore the law and continued to issue orders outside his jurisdiction, including an amended order dismissing the remaining five claims! He was not only ignoring his responsibility, he was attempting to clean up his sloppy May 5th dismissal that excluded five of the claims.

Flanagan was shameless in this high profile case. But he knew, like UNR knew, and I had been learning, that the *Reno Gazette Journal* – in their brazen and biased efforts to protect UNR – would not expose him.

Jeff immediately brought this judicial misconduct to the attention of the Chief Judge of the Court, Judge Steinheimer. Steinheimer transferred the case temporarily to Judge Brent Adams to hear the motion to disqualify. In the meantime, Judge Flanagan refused to vacate the orders that were undeniably issued outside his jurisdiction.

Moore v. District Court, 364 P.2d 1073 Nev. (1961) reads in part:

> An order issued after the filing of the affidavit of prejudice "has no validity."

On May 26, 2009, the motion to disqualify Judge Flanagan was denied by Judge Brent Adams after a hearing on the same day. The allegations of bias that we brought forth were undisputed because Judge Flanagan had not filed a response as he was required to do – and he failed to show at the hearing. This was just another embarrassing clown act in the circus that was the Washoe County courthouse.

Although Mary Dugan had a vested interest in the disqualification motion – her close personal relationship with Flanagan was at issue – it was noteworthy that Dugan failed to appear at the May 26, 2009, hearing clearly dodging the dilemma of having to answer to this allegation.

Despite the fact that the procedures were not followed by Judge Flanagan and the bias allegations were unopposed – oh and that tiny little issue that the law mandated disqualification based on the Beattie issue alone – Judge Adams denied our motion.

But *Foster v. Dingwall*, 227 P.3d 1042 Nev. (2010) says Judge Adams was wrong:

> A party's failure to oppose a motion "constitutes an admission that the motion was meritorious."

Several months later, in another UNR case, Judge Adams would admit to several long-standing affiliations – and conflicts of interest – with the university. He subsequently recused himself from that case. By his own belated admission, he should never have presided over the motion to disqualify Judge Flanagan in my case.

*   *   *

While my case was now on appeal to the Nevada Supreme Court, my administrative reinstatement case was still bouncing around between the DOP and the district court – albeit at a snail's pace. Nearly one year after we had unsuccessfully tried to disqualify Judge Flanagan from my main case, my appeal for my reinstatement case landed before – you guessed it – Judge Flanagan. So, on June 14, 2010, I moved to disqualify Flanagan from my reinstatement appeal. And if we were fortunate enough to have this disqualification affirmed by another district judge, Flanagan would assuredly be off both cases. Could I be so lucky?!

The same procedures were in play. But this time, I was representing myself in this matter. Why? Because – on this issue of reinstatement – I knew the facts better than anyone, and I was also chomping at the bit to depose Judge Flanagan in open court. But I doubted that he would show up and give me such satisfaction. After I filed the affidavit of bias Flanagan surprisingly filed an answer to my allegations, and he showed up at the motion hearing that would be heard by Judge Jerry Polaha. It was me and Judge Flanagan in a public courtroom – with the "Judge" on the witness stand and the soccer coach deposing him. How in the hell did I end up here?!

The courtroom filled with several onlookers who must have heard that there was a coach deposing a judge in Department 3. University lawyers Robison and Hilsabeck were visibly unnerved while Mary Dugan was hiding out in her office on the UNR campus. She left her friend, Judge Flanagan, to face the firing squad of one by himself.

In addition to presenting the same bias allegations addressed a year earlier, I surprised Judge Flanagan when I suddenly produced a copy of his wife Caroline's public Facebook profile. The profile revealed that she had a "friendship" with Dan Dugan, Mary Dugan's husband. Upon receiving the copy of his wife's Facebook profile, Judge Flanagan turned several shades of red while searching the ceiling for answers. Unfortunately for him, the ceiling did not provide any assistance. But later that evening Caroline Flanagan removed her profile from Facebook. I am sure that they had an interesting conversation at dinner that evening.

Oddly enough, a year earlier, Caroline Flanagan was seen peeking through the door from the judge's chambers into the courtroom during the April 2009 hearings in my main case. It seemed my case was a family affair for the Flanagans as well as for the Dugans.

In the days immediately following this exposure of Caroline Flanagan's public profile, President Glick, AD Cary Groth, and Mary Dugan's husband, Dan, all privatized their Facebook profiles in unison. The UNR administration should have paid attention to the old adage that the cover-up is always worse than the crime. I've often wondered if the big Operation Facebook meeting was held on campus at taxpayers' expense.

Back to the hearing. While under oath, and in response to my questioning, Judge Flanagan admitted to being long-time close personal friends with the Dugans. In describing his social relationship with the

Dugans, he said that he regularly played tennis with Dan Dugan – prior to his accident that caused his paralysis. Judge Flanagan also admitted that he had a business relationship with Dan Dugan and that he had spent time with Dan Dugan in Dan's office while my case was pending before him. It stretches the limits of credulity to believe that the subject of this "high profile case" wasn't touched upon during their discourse.

So after I forced him to spill the beans on his relationship with the Dugans, I began zeroing in on all of the fraud he had committed against me in dismissing my main case. I had him under oath on the witness stand for two hours under the watchful eye of several spectators. Robison and Hilsabeck squirmed throughout but they could not intercede. This was between me and the "Judge."

In what was a stunning admission, Judge Flanagan testified that he had written and submitted his answer to my affidavit of bias without reading my affidavit!

Q My first question to you would be did you read my affidavit?
A No
Q You did have the opportunity to read it?
A I had the opportunity. I did not read it.
Q You did not read it?
A No.

This admission proved that he issued rulings not based on the record before him; a flagrant violation of the US Constitution. Is this the proper way for a district judge to conduct himself in a legal proceeding? The man did not read the complaint of bias filed against himself and even seemed to be proud of it. If he didn't think enough of the law to follow it, it seems he would have been curious about the complaints against him so he could at least attempt to defend himself against them. More evidence of Flanagan's lack of propriety and incompetence will be provided in the next chapter.

As I continued to grill him about his misconduct in my main case, he had to regret that he ever showed up at the hearing. In addition to a number of admissions I was able to drag out of him, he also lied several times while on the witness stand.

Judge Flanagan admitted that he had a conflict of interest in cases that involved his former client Craig Beattie. Flanagan further testified that he had recused himself from another case that involved Beattie because "pursuant to the canons, I felt it would have been improper for me to continue to hear the matter."

> Q And you admitted today that you recused yourself from the
> Grand Jury petition because of your involvement with Craig
> Beatty [sic]?
>
> A I did.

Judge Flanagan then testified falsely three times under oath by claiming that my attorney – Jeff – had waived Flanagan's conflict with Beattie in my main case. Here's the exchange between the "Judge" and me:

> Q . . . there was a Motion in Limine that Doctor Hussein was going
> to **testify on matters pertaining to his retaliation suffered
> by your former client Craig Beatty** [sic]. Under the Nevada
> judicial canons and under your own testimony right there you
> are required to be disqualified if you had served as a lawyer in
> matters of controversy.
>
> A . . . I will say that as soon as I got this case I disclosed my
> representation of Craig Beatty [sic]. And [Jeff] and I had a
> **colloquy on the record in the transcript in which he waived
> any conflict.** I made sure that both – that all parties knew . . .
> And when this case again came in front of me I made sure that
> that the [Beattie] relationship was disclosed on the record. And
> it was discussed. **And any conflict was waived.**
>
> Q And what record was that on?
>
> A **It is in the transcript of the first hearing.** When they
> brought – referred to me by the Chief Judge. **It occurred at the
> first hearing we had in this case . . .** and, as I said, I made sure
> I had the – that relationship on the record. **And it was – it was
> waived. And I can provide a copy of the transcript today.**

Unsurprisingly, Judge Flanagan failed to provide a copy of the transcript supporting his statements. He didn't produce the transcript because it proved that not only was there no waiver for the Beattie conflict, he had never sought one. The transcript would have also demonstrated that he had lied under oath about the waiver's existence. And by broaching the subject of the waiver, he was admitting that such waiver was required.

Judge Polaha was clearly bewildered by what he was witnessing in his courtroom. I am confident that, despite his number of years on the bench, he had never had a coach depose a judge in his presence before. Because he was seemingly engrossed in what was unfolding before him, he, much to my surprise, put no limits on me or my line of questioning.

As this very public deposition of Judge Flanagan was coming to a close, Judge Polaha – astonished that Judge Flanagan would endure such public humiliation – blurted out:

JUDGE POLAHA: You have to wonder why he just doesn't say, "Hey, this is it. I'm out of here."

Exactly. Why didn't he have enough sense to see that he was losing the battle and retreat before he made a bigger fool of himself?

The obvious answer was that something was happening that wasn't supposed to happen in America. A judge was siding with one team in a legal proceeding – and it was abundantly clear that he wasn't a teammate of mine.

*   *   *

At the conclusion of the hearing, Judge Polaha asked me to submit some additional information to him in writing in the following days. But I am certain I gave him more than he had asked for. In an August 14, 2010, motion I submitted direct evidence of Judge Flanagan's bias and judicial misconduct as enumerated above, detailing the number of times the "Judge" had committed perjury in his presence at the hearing. I reminded Judge Polaha of not only his obligation to disqualify Flanagan, but also of his obligation to report Judge Flanagan to the Committee on Judicial Discipline; a committee on which Judge Polaha served. Judge Flanagan had put Judge Polaha in an untenable position.

After fifteen months and all our efforts to get Judge Flanagan off my cases, on August 26, 2010, while my main case was still on appeal and pending before the Nevada Supreme Court, Judge Flanagan recused himself – from both my reinstatement appeal and my main case

– before Judge Polaha issued his order. I was ecstatic! He was finally gone. And then I read his order of recusal and burst out laughing at how small-minded this man truly was. While claiming his recusal was 'voluntary', the embarrassed judge lashed out at me – accusing me of 'violating his family's privacy' because I had printed his wife's public Facebook profile from the Internet. Apparently the "Judge" believed that there was an expectation of privacy for publicly posted material on the world-wide-web.

It was a desperate attempt to save face – but an embarrassing one at that by this so-called "Judge" in Reno, Nevada.

* * *

All orders issued after April 28, 2009 – the day that Flanagan's representation of Dr. Craig Beattie first became an issue in my case – are void because they were issued by a judge without jurisdiction. This important law deserves repeating, *Hoff v. Eighth Judicial District Court*, 378 P.2d 977 Nev. (1963):

> The actions of a district judge who is disqualified by statute are not voidable merely, but **void**.

And in *Turner v. State*, 962 P.2d 1223 Nev. (1998):

> It would be inconsistent with these goals to apply a harmless error analysis to a judge's improper failure to recuse himself . . . such failure mandates automatic reversal.

Because of his recusal, a new judge would be assigned to my case once the Nevada Supreme Court reversed his ridiculous dismissal of my 19 claims. I only needed one claim to be reversed and I would get my well overdue day in front of a jury of my peers.

CHAPTER 16

Juice Town

"I consider trial by jury as the only anchor ever yet imagined by man, by which a government can be held to the principles of its Constitution."
~ Thomas Jefferson, 1789

A high-profile attorney decided to join my team and take on my case at no cost to me. Attorneys of his stature do not make such a gesture unless they determine, based on the evidence, that the case is a winner. In 2007-08, five women brought retaliation claims against Fresno State University and its athletic department, resulting in over $20 million dollars in damages to the university. FSU lost two of the cases at jury trial and settled the other three out of court. Dan Siegel, a California attorney, successfully represented all five women. Four months from trial, in January of 2009, Dan and his wife Ann, who is also a lawyer and was involved in the FSU cases, both joined my team.

Dan shared with me encouraging words a couple of months after he had familiarized himself with my case: "After reviewing the entire record I do not know how the university is possibly going to defend this case." Of course, I agreed with him but the words from such an esteemed lawyer were manna from heaven.

Dan was astounded that we had been able to secure voluntary admissions of retaliation from Groth. Dan had a tremendous reputation as a trial lawyer and Jeff welcomed Dan and Anne into the fold. Jeff, Dan, Anne, and I all knew my case was a slam-dunk, even more so with our new line-up. The evidence was overwhelmingly in my favor and we all agreed that there was no way the university could ever let the case go to trial. Even though the defense might push the envelope and allow the case to proceed closer and closer to the trial date, I felt confident that in the eleventh hour they would settle.

The only caveat to this ideal scenario was that they wouldn't have "the judge in their pocket."

But of course, as demonstrated in the previous chapter, that was exactly what they wound up having. And if that judge was removed, there was another one right behind him waiting to take his place. But as for Judge Flanagan, he was not only in their pocket he had no jurisdiction to sit in judgment of my case. But there was no oversight; no grand authority existed that would hold him accountable to the laws that govern our society. Dan and Anne were accustomed to a justice system in California that adhered to the law and held their judges up to stringent and rigorous standards. Dan, a savvy and sophisticated individual, had undoubtedly heard of the less than stellar record of the Nevada judicial system. However, he had no idea just how pervasive and deep its "injustice" ran, and that the law of the old Wild West was alive and well in Washoe County, Nevada.

In addition to Judge Flanagan's involvement with Dugan, Reid, and Beattie, another question lingered about the other judges who worked in the same courthouse. Would it be feasible to suspect that one or more of his colleagues, who all had admitted conflicts of interest with the university and/or its officials, walked a few steps down the hall to Judge Flanagan's office and encouraged him to throw out my case? We'll never know but our suspicions were warranted and grounded in facts not in our imagination.

Of the eight judges assigned to the Washoe County District Court, six had biases leaning toward the home team – the University of Nevada:

- Judge Steve Elliot's wife was a member of the AAUN Board of Directors; the couple was a donor and supporter of the athletic department
- Judge Janet Berry's husband was a "very large donor" to Nevada athletics

- o Judge Robert Perry admitted to a friendship with General Counsel Mary Dugan and recused himself from at least two UNR cases because of it
- o Judge Brent Adams admitted to a number of conflicts with the university
- o Judge Jerry Polaha was a former football player at Nevada and was a donor to the athletic department
- o Judge Flanagan – Please see Chapter 15

Judge Flanagan's bias played out in the disturbing order he handed down. He dismissed my case, and in so doing, it would not be a stretch to say that he altered the entire record that was before him. His order was a fabrication that bore no connection whatsoever to the evidence.

All the evidence laid out in previous chapters was pre-existing before my encounter with Judge Flanagan. He had the evidence that the university and its administrators fabricated documents, committed perjury, tampered with evidence and witnesses, solicited student-athletes to manufacture evidence, and, of course most salient of all, admitted to acts of retaliation. The university never once denied that they committed these criminal acts. They couldn't because the evidence was indisputable. Instead they just ignored the mound of evidence exposing their fraud hoping that it would go away. Since that was not going to happen without help, Judge Flanagan came to their rescue.

I will share with you some of the judge's most outrageous fabrications in his order of dismissal. As shown by his own testimony in the previous chapter, Judge Flanagan admitted to issuing rulings without reading the record before him. That same contemptible behavior is illustrated here.

* * *

When UNR filed its "motion for *partial* summary judgment", the university was asking the judge to dismiss some of the claims in my case. But the motion was filed four days past the deadline, which was in direct violation of the court's scheduling order. Team Dugan offered no excuse for their tardiness, and the scheduling order said that "except upon a showing of unforeseen extraordinary circumstances, the Court will not entertain any pretrial motions filed . . . after the . . . deadlines have passed." So in response, we filed a motion to strike their belated summary judgment filing. To assist his friends at the university, Judge Flanagan simply ignored our motion to strike and allowed their motion to carry.

*　　*　　*

Judge Flanagan wrote a lengthy, detailed commentary – fully one and one-half pages – that contained his duly considered rationale in dismissing "my Title IX sexual harassment claim." One huge problem with that – *I never filed a sexual harassment claim!* A judge's order is supposed to be based on the briefing before him. But, appropriately, neither party briefed this claim because it did not exist. This proved that Flanagan had not based his order on the record of the case and that he, once again, had not read the briefing! Instead, in his eagerness to dismiss my case, Flanagan chose to review the brief that resided only in his head. Judge Flanagan manufactured hundreds of words out of thin air to dismiss a make-believe claim. The words, "corrupt", "incompetent" "sexist" and "humiliating" all rush at me when I recall the incident. With this astonishing blunder coupled with his admitted failure to read my affidavit of bias, the judge was certainly establishing an alarming pattern that did not do justice to the very justice system that he represented.

*　　*　　*

As shown in the last chapter, Flanagan threw out the last five claims without notice to me. Under my right to due process and supporting case law, he acted without authority. Because there was no briefing in the record to support his action, he had to manufacture reasons in writing for dismissing these claims. *Idaho Resources v. Freeport-McMoran*, 874 P.2d 742 (1994):

> The district court is not authorized to enter judgment on a claim which has not been presented to the court for resolution and has not been briefed or argued . . . [A] trial court has no authority to render a decision on issues not presented for determination. Any findings rendered outside the issues are a nullity.

*   *   *

Since this was an employment case UNR had to proffer a legal basis for ending my employment. UNR could not submit Groth's deposition because it contained her admission of retaliation for my report of facility inequities among the male and female athletes. They had nothing. And that's what they submitted – nothing. As a result Judge Flanagan in an act of judicial fiat *created* a basis to support Groth's unconscionable decision that was entirely unsupported by *any* evidence and had no connection to reality.

*   *   *

In dismissing my Title VII Equal Protection Claim, the judge once again blatantly altered the record before him. He wrote that Jeff "admitted at oral argument that there was **no direct evidence** showing unlawful discrimination." But the exact opposite was true. The record shows that Jeff stated that there was direct evidence of unlawful discrimination at least *eight* separate times at the April 20, 2009, oral argument. For example – Jeff argued:

> Plaintiff's equal protection claim should advance to trial. There's **direct evidence** that her reporting discrimination caused her termination . . . it was a motivating factor, **direct evidence** . . .

> It's **direct evidence** of the reporting activity upon which we base our retaliation claim of the equal protection clause and under Title VII . . .

*   *   *

In dismissing my "tortuous inference with contract" claim, Judge Flanagan wrote:

> There is **no factual dispute** here that Ms. Groth was **not** a party to [my] contract with UNR.

But UNR argued that Groth **was** a party to the contract. We argued that Groth was **not** a party to the contract. Clearly there was a factual dispute, and – under the law – this factual dispute could only be decided by a jury. Because of this, Judge Flanagan altered the record to ensure a jury never had a chance.

*   *   *

In dismissing my Title IX retaliation claim, in the original May 5th, order he dismissed it based on a rationale under a case called *Garcetti v. Ceballos*. But that case has nothing whatsoever to do with a Title IX claim. So realizing the *Garcetti* case was grossly misplaced here – when he issued the amended order on May 18th to throw out the remaining five claims – he *created* and slipped in a new rationale to justify dismissal of my Title IX claim. He realized the embarrassing gaffe he had committed and was making a feeble attempt to cover himself.

*   *   *

Judge Flanagan ignored the three direct admissions of retaliation:

"She was not paid more because she complained or allegedly spoke freely about Title IX and NCAA infractions."

_____

"Terri you're a great, great coach. Nobody can deny that. I just need to move on. I looked in your personnel file. There was nothing to use against you."

"This has whistleblower retaliation written all over it," I responded.

"I know," replied Groth.

_____

I highly recommend that Mr. Norcross be given a long lesson on the consequences of gender inequity in higher education. His lack of respect for the female student-athletes and staff at Nevada has the makings of a very expensive proposition for this university.

In response to my memorandum about facility inequities, Groth testified in her deposition:

Q Why did you terminate Terri?
A . . . If we didn't talk to the – if we didn't handle the facility situations, she would threaten that it would cost millions of – or a lot of money.

Any one of these admissions *guaranteed* me my day in court before a jury of my peers. The judge ignored all three to make sure that never happened.

*   *   *

The eleventh hour was approaching and just as I and my legal team had speculated, less than two weeks before trial the university offered me $150,000 to settle the case. While that is certainly a lot of money in most contexts, it came nowhere near the figure needed to repair the damage they had caused. The offer was not made in good faith and Robison even admitted that he knew I would not accept it. Jeff notified Dan, Anne, and I of the offer but we didn't waste any time even considering it.

In addition to fabricating the entire case record to dismiss my case, adding insult to injury, Flanagan brazenly issued an order stating that I had to pay UNR $111,000 for their attorneys' fees! Of course the university has never tried to collect on this judgment because they knew it was invalid. It was a 'void' order because it was issued after April 28, 2009, when Judge Flanagan lost jurisdiction to sit in judgment of this case. **A void judgment is one which has no legal force or effect whatever, it is an absolute nullity** (*Black's Law Dictionary*).

The basis behind the order of attorneys' fees was obvious. Neither the judge nor UNR expected me to ever pay; they just wanted to intimidate me into settling the case and not proceeding on to an appellate court. The settlement would be structured like this: I drop the case and they would waive the $111,000. But despite their desire to enter settlement talks at this point, we were not interested. We knew what was coming and it would only be a waste of time.

Judge Flanagan was guilty of judicial misconduct but still sits on the bench in Reno, Nevada. His flagrant disregard for the law and his offhanded dismissal of the compelling evidence that was submitted before him begs the question: Why was he so comfortable in abandoning his oath of office in this high-profile case, and why was he unconcerned about any reprisal or recrimination for his actions?

The answer was simple: when it came down to juice vs. justice, Reno, Nevada, was a juice town.

CHAPTER 17

Avalanche of Lies

"The supreme quality for leadership is unquestionably integrity. Without it, no real success is possible, no matter whether it is on a section gang, a football field, in an army, or in an office."

~ Dwight D. Eisenhower

While my case was on appeal to the Nevada Supreme Court, the university repeatedly asked for extensions of time to file their brief. Since they knew they could never win on the merits, they were dragging it out as long as possible. Their delay tactics had a dual goal: to wear me down and compel me to quit; and, to have as much time as possible to continue their nefarious behind-the-scenes work.

Despite what I had been through, I held out hope that my case would be treated fairly in the highest court in Nevada's judicial system. Although I had hope I can't say I was surprised that we had no better luck in the Nevada Supreme Court in finding justices who were without conflicts of interest with the university and NSHE. The close and incestuous environment that was pervasive in the lower courts ran rampant in the state's highest court as well. It was simply incredible that of the seven Supreme Court justices in Nevada, there was not one without conflicts of interest in my case.

Despite the fact that Mary Dugan and Kent Robison had known for over six weeks that Justice Kristina Pickering was assigned to the case, they waited until just five days prior to oral argument to file a "Notice of

Disclosure" of Justice Pickering's conflicts of interest. Robison had been representing Justice Pickering's husband, who was also a lawyer, for over 16 months. After Robison filed the notice of disclosure, Justice Pickering immediately recused herself. It is remarkable that this notice was even necessary since she was responsible for revealing her own conflicts. Why did she have to be prodded into doing the right thing? I was faced with the same reality that I had unwittingly grown accustomed to in the lower courts: the justices who were elected to hold the public trust were not to be trusted. I hoped that I had stepped off the merry-go-round when I left the district court system but it seemed that I was still spinning.

But the disclosure was a curious tactic by the defense. With all their high jinks and machinations during the long legal process, why was the university suddenly so forthright about Pickering's conflict? It was a move that was decidedly out of character for Team Dugan. They had never before bothered to disclose any conflicts; in fact, they went out of their way to conceal them. Were they worried that Justice Pickering would not be an ally even though Robison was her husband's attorney? It ultimately became clear that the main reason they forced Justice Pickering off the case was because it was court practice that the Chief Justice would be called upon to replace any recused judge. And the Chief Justice at the time was none other than Nancy Saitta whose dubious judicial career, you will recall, I already devoted an entire chapter to. Saitta had been named the Chief Justice of the Nevada Supreme Court in September 2011, one month before my case was to be heard. Dugan et al. apparently had more faith in Justice Saitta's favorable participation in the case than they did in Pickering's.

Justice James Hardesty – a UNR alumnus – recused himself, but only after I disclosed his involvement with Nevada athletics. Again, Hardesty didn't divulge his conflicts forthrightly as he was required to do. Hardesty was up to his ears in the university. We learned that he, too, was a significant donor and had given so much to the university that he qualified as a "Golden Wolf" – an elite status for big donors. He had also served on several committees for Pack PAWS, an organization that supported women's athletics at Nevada.

Hardesty and Pickering were the only two who stepped aside. Of course, they did not go willingly and had to be nudged out. But the other five justices sat on my case despite their own conflicts of interest with NSHE.

Justice Michael Cherry was also a donor to NSHE (UNLV athletics) which was a direct conflict of interest according to the Nevada Code of Judicial Conduct which states in part: " . . . a judge *shall not* participate in activities that would appear to a reasonable person to undermine the judge's independence, integrity, or impartiality."

In spite of the rules and laws that governed judicial recusals, there was no authority over the justices that held them accountable. While my case was pending before the Nevada Supreme Court, a brunch and tribute was held honoring current NSHE/UNR staff member and Athletic Director Emeritus Dick Trachok. Members of UNR's administration, including the defendants, were in attendance and the event was promoted on the Nevada athletic department website. It was widely reported in the media that "several justices" of the Nevada Supreme also attended this function. Socializing with parties to a case during its pendency would appear to any "reasonable person to undermine the justice's independence and impartiality." But again the justices were allowed to violate the rules of the Nevada Code of Judicial Conduct with impunity.

An annual athletic department event called the "Governor's Dinner" was promoted as the "premier fund raising event of the year" for Nevada Wolf Pack athletics. Joe Bradley, President of the AAUN, and Associate AD Rory Hickok sent several emails about securing a speaker for the Governor's Dinner that upcoming summer. One email describing the event read in part:

> By way of background, the Governor's Dinner has been a tradition in Northern Nevada for many years, this will be the 41st annual dinner. It is held in the back yard of the Governor's Mansion in Carson City . . . Unless his schedule absolutely precludes his attendance, the Governor is there, as well as many other distinguished Nevadan's including State Senator Raggio, **U.S. Senators Reid** and Ensign, **members of the Nevada Supreme Court** and numerous influential Northern Nevada business, education and community leaders.

This meant that AD Groth sent invitations directly to the justices while our case was before them! It also meant that Groth, UNR President Milton Glick, UNR General Counsel Mary Dugan, and Robison and Arrascada – who were Wolf Pack donors – were socializing with the justices of the Nevada Supreme Court at the defendants' "premier fund raising event of the year." The justices either received a gift of the $300 ticket – or $600 if they brought a guest – or each attending justice paid for the tickets and thus made a donation to Nevada athletics. In either instance, their participation in this event made them a "representative[s] of Nevada's athletics interests" or in layman's terms, donors to Nevada athletics. This bears repeating: " . . . a judge *shall not* participate in activities that would appear to a reasonable person to undermine the judge's independence, integrity, or impartiality."

According to the United States Supreme Court:

If a judge knows something that others in the case do not know, and it would cause an appearance of bias, he has an obligation to *identify it* and *get out of the case." Liljeberg v. Health Svcs. Acq. Corp*, 486 U.S. 847 (1988).

The US Supreme Court called a judge's failure to do so "inexcusable." The justices of the Nevada Supreme Court concealed their social activities with the defendants and remained on my case. We had even filed a motion asking them to disclose which justices attended these functions with the defendants. They didn't deny that several justices were in attendance but refused to disclose which ones attended. This concealment in clear violation of established law demonstrated that the justices recognized that they were in the wrong. "Justice must satisfy the appearance of justice," *Levine v. United States*, 362 U.S. 610, 80 S. Ct. 1038 (1960).

Nevada's own case law recognized and cited to US Supreme Court precedent on the importance of an unbiased judiciary. In *re Ross*, 656 P.2d 832 Nev. (1983) the Nevada Supreme Court wrote:

The United States Supreme Court has made it clear that "[t]he Due Process Clause entitles a person to an impartial and disinterested tribunal in both civil and criminal cases." *Marshall v. Jerrico, Inc.*, 446 U.S. 238, 242, 100 S.Ct. 1610,1613, 64 L.Ed.2d 182 (1980). It has further said: "Not only is a biased decision maker constitutionally unacceptable but ʻour system of law has always endeavored to prevent even the probability of unfairness.'" *Withrow v. Larkin*, 421 U.S. 35,

48, 95 S.Ct. 1456,1465, 43 L.Ed.2d 712 (1974); *Gibson v. Berryhill*, 411 U.S. 564, 93 S.Ct. 1689, 36 L.Ed.2d 488 (1973).

It looks good. It sounds great. But as I had come to learn, in Nevada, those entrusted to uphold the law were some of its worst violators.

*   *   *

After Robison curiously forced Justice Pickering's recusal a *Notice of Disclosure* detailing Justice Saitta's many conflicts of interest was filed on my behalf. I had connected the dots between her and NSHE and other key players involved in my case. The notice detailed Saitta's prior employment and current involvement with NSHE and other interested parties.

Despite the fact that these conflicts *far exceeded* those of Justice Pickering and Justice Hardesty, both of whom had recused themselves, Justice Saitta refused to voluntarily declare them and remove herself from my appeal. No one who had the authority to do so – her colleagues on the bench – challenged her non-action. Justice Saitta did not deny these conflicts; rather, she concealed them from the public by refusing to file the *"Notice of Disclosure"* on the docket. In addition to her previous employment with NSHE, Justice Saitta had been working on behalf of and with NSHE throughout the pendency of my appeal. Saitta's failure to disclose her conflicts of interest was evidence of bias in and of itself.

To illustrate Saitta's continued relationship with NSHE, just two weeks prior to the commencement of oral argument in my case, Justice Saitta partnered with NSHE in "Step Up For Kids", a campaign to raise awareness for children's issues. Chief Justice Saitta was also a presenter at an NSHE sponsored event on the UNLV campus. NSHE promoted Justice Saitta on its website. The University of Nevada, Reno issued a press release on its website promoting Justice Saitta's scheduled appearance as a speaker at a continuing education course on an NSHE campus. The event was sponsored by NSHE institutions UNR and UNLV. Chief Justice Saitta spoke and moderated this continuing education course on behalf of NSHE.

In her appearances as a presenter, speaker and moderator at these NSHE sponsored events during the pendency of my appeal, Justice Saitta was acting as an instructor on NSHE's campuses. NSHE promoted

Justice Saitta on multiple websites while my appeal was before her. It was clear that Saitta was in regular communication with NSHE officials to schedule and coordinate her involvement at these various events on NSHE's behalf.

Prior to becoming a judge, Saitta was employed in private practice by Gentile and Porter. Dominic Gentile, then a partner in the firm, was a Las Vegas attorney and adjunct professor for NSHE and participated in the continuing education course with Justice Saitta. Gentile was also a member of the Nevada Supreme Court Bench-Bar Committee where he interacted with the justices. Gentile's law firm had been a substantial contributor to Justice Saitta's election campaigns. Gentile was also a colleague and personal friend of Attorney John Arrascada, Groth's personal attorney. And, I learned later that, since 2007, Gentile worked for Gordon Silver, whose Las Vegas firm had been conducting research on me while my case was on appeal before the Nevada Supreme Court.

At the October 31, 2011, oral argument, Chief Justice Saitta entered the room and smiled and nodded her head directly at Arrascada in what I considered a disturbing and inappropriate exchange. The overt friendliness displayed between Saitta and defense counsel throughout oral argument was suspect and left little doubt in my mind that the outcome had been decided before Saitta even set foot in the courtroom.

Justice Saitta was on the Board of Directors of the *Public Education Foundation*. She was re-elected to the board on October 27, 2011, four days before commencement of oral argument in my case. NSHE Chancellor Emeritus Jim Rogers was also on the Board of Directors of the same foundation. Rogers was the active Chancellor of NSHE when I initiated my claims against Groth, Glick, and NSHE. He continues to this day his public advocacy of NSHE.

Rory Reid, who is the son of Senator Reid and the brother of Cindy Fox's wayward attorney Leif Reid, was also on the Board of Directors of the *Public Education Foundation*. Rory Reid is a long-time supporter of Justice Saitta and, according to published reports, had encouraged her to run for U.S. Congress in 2005.

Judges are the gatekeepers to jurisprudence, to the Constitution, to access to the courts and to due process. But clearly this was not a fair and even playing field. In what had grown into a multi-million dollar case, five justices of the Nevada Supreme Court turned blind eyes to the corruption that had permeated my case throughout every step of the process.

For the Supreme Court to fairly affirm the dismissal of all 19 claims in my case, the justices would have had to declare that constitutional rights were irrelevant within Nevada's borders. The justices should have overturned the lower court order just on the district court judge's lack of jurisdiction alone. But that didn't happen. My suspicions that Chief Justice Saitta was just going through the motions and had a preconceived opinion were ultimately confirmed.

The order issued by the Nevada Supreme Court – which affirmed a complete dismissal – was devoid of *any* evidentiary support and wholly contradicted by the record. The following is a sampling of the court's errors that resulted in a grievous miscarriage of justice.

*   *   *

The right to be heard is a constitutional guarantee established to ensure a fair process of decision-making. "Being heard" required that the justices read and based their decision on the briefing presented to them. But we had clear proof at the outset that they had not read our briefs prior to issuing their order affirming the case's dismissal. Previously, on October 25, 2010, the justices had "granted judicial notice" of Judge Flanagan's belated recusal from my case, and of the NCAA's sanctions against the university (more on that later). Both of these facts had occurred after we filed our initial statement of appeal. So by motion we had asked the court to recognize these belated but established facts. Several months later, in our briefing, we reminded them that they had already "granted judicial notice" of these facts:

> On October 25, 2010, this Court granted the motion: "appellant's unopposed request for judicial notice is granted." *October 25. 2010, Order.*

But in their order affirming dismissal of my case they wrote: the court "declines to take judicial notice" . . . of the very same facts for which it had already "granted judicial notice" of! It was painfully obvious that they had not read the briefing or reviewed the case docket or they would not have issued an order contradicting an order they had already issued. Additionally, in their order they repeatedly referred to Judge Flanagan as the judge of record – even sending him a copy of the final order – despite the fact that it had been made abundantly clear in the briefing that Flanagan had been removed from the case.

*   *   *

It became more and more obvious that the justices were on a mission to kill my case. In affirming the dismissal of my Title IX claim, they wrote:

> While Patraw argues that NSHE admitted retaliation in termination or pay, Patraw does not identify anywhere in the record where NSHE made such an admission. Thus Patraw fails to establish retaliation by direct evidence.

But we identified in the record the direct admissions of retaliation **18** times! Would 19 times have done the job? Or 20? What was the magic number?!

On page six of our opening brief we identified and cited to the record the first admission of retaliation:

> Terri you're a great, great coach. Nobody can deny that. I just need to move on. I looked in your personnel file. There was nothing to use against you. *JA III, 556:19 to 557:1.*

On page 21 of our opening brief – under a heading titled "**Defendants Admitted Retaliation in Pay**" – we wrote and cited to the record:

> Defendants admitted that Patraw "was not paid more because she complained or allegedly spoke freely about Title IX and NCAA infractions." *JA II, 458:11-12.*

On page 19, there was another can't-miss heading titled "**Groth Admitted Termination Was Retaliation for Title IX Speech.**" And in support of this we detailed her direct admission that she retaliated against me for addressing the inequitable facility issues on behalf of my female athletes. There were 16 other references to Groth and NSHE's direct admissions of retaliation sprinkled throughout the briefing. But regardless, I only needed one. And clearly I had that. On one admission alone, my case should have gone to trial with the availability of unlimited damages under Title IX.

The justices didn't attempt subtlety in their misconduct and their ineptitude was palpable. When we later filed a petition for rehearing – which asked them to reconsider their order due to clear error – we again pointed out by page and line number each and every one of the 18 citations. But the justices ignored it all and denied the petition for rehearing with a single word – DENIED.

*   *   *

UNR finally conceded to the Nevada Supreme Court that Groth had offered me a multi-year contract extension six days before I left Nevada. Prior to this admission, Groth had lied under oath denying that she had offered me the contract.

Groth had testified in her deposition:

Q   Had the 2.5-year contract offer been extended to her?
A   No. There's never been – I've never had a discussion with Terri on a multi-year contract.

Despite overwhelming evidence to the contrary, Dugan and Robison had also argued in front of Judge Flanagan that I was *not* offered the 2.5-year contract in August 2007. At the April 2009, oral argument, Dugan insisted that no such offer was made:

DUGAN: . . . Jeff was trying to say that there was assurances from Athletic Director Groth **in August that Patraw . . . would get a long-term contract. That's simply not true** . . .

So regardless of the fact that **there might have been some discussion of a possible contract for longer than a year** at the beginning of the meeting, at the end of the meeting **everybody knew that no one was sure they wanted to move forward at all**. So there's no assurances of long-term employment.

But clearly at the end of the August meeting, **there were no assurances either way that there was going to be any continued discussion about a multi-year contract**, even for more than one year.

General Counsel Dugan's credibility was impeached by her own letter to my attorney Marc on September 5, 2007:

[Patraw] refused the contract offer that was made to her on August 22, 2007, in a meeting with A.D. Groth.

Additionally, five other university officials and employees, including the provost and assistant VP of HR, all testified that I was offered the 2.5-year contract. I also had a copy of the offer in my possession. Despite all this evidence before the district court, Robison continued the willful misrepresentation of the record:

ROBISON: And **you're quite correct, your Honor, there's no offer** for any contract at any stated salary. There are negotiations. She's on a one-year contract, June of 2007, yes, **we indulge her for discussions. We didn't offer her any extended contract or anything of the nature**.

But years later – in 2011 – in their brief to the Nevada Supreme Court, Dugan and Robison admitted that "**NSHE . . . offered her another appointment for 2.5 years with a raise, which Patraw rejected**." This was an admission that they outright lied to the district court to conceal the retaliation. After all, it would be inconceivable to dismiss a coach coming off a championship season just six days after offering her an extension and raise. That would never make it past a jury.

It is the principle of evidence law that the fact-finder is entitled to treat a party's dishonesty about a material fact as affirmative evidence of guilt. *Reeves v. Sanderson's Plumb. Prod., Inc.*, 530 U.S. 133, 147 (2000).

With this admission, the university admitted that Groth had committed perjury and that NSHE had committed fraud in the district court; and it changed its position on a key issue in my case. On the second point, the law does not allow a position change on appeal; the record on appeal must remain exactly as it was when submitted. The Supreme Court chose to ignore this law, too. And in addition to ignoring Groth's perjury, the justices failed to sanction Robison and Dugan for their intentionally false statements to the district court.

* * *

Team Dugan had not provided any evidence in the district court to support a non-retaliatory reason for ending my employment. So as I detailed in the previous chapter, Judge Flanagan cured their deficiencies, fabricating a basis on their behalf. We articulated the university's shortcomings in our briefing to the Nevada Supreme Court. In response, the university cited to Judge Flanagan's order as their evidence. In other words, they sheepishly admitted that the only evidence they had was Judge Flanagan's order! But a court order is NOT evidence. Evidence is testimony and documents submitted by the parties. And it is that evidence that is supposed to form the findings in the order. But because there was no evidence that supported the 'findings' in Judge Flanagan's order, the fabricated order was all Team Dugan had to cite to. And Groth herself had also famously admitted that she looked in my personnel file and had nothing to use against me. The Supreme Court was briefed on all of this but, in order to protect their social friends at UNR from liability, they too manufactured a basis to cure UNR's deficiencies. They wrote:

> Off the field, Patraw was involved in conflicts with other coaches that included professional and personal matters.

But the evidence in the record showed just the opposite; I was rated by the university as "commendable" for "interpersonal relationships." Comments like "supports colleagues and other programs well", "a team player", and "communicates well with administration and support staff" were documented throughout my personnel file and the case briefing. There was not a single negative mark against me anywhere in the record of the case. The justices decided that Team Dugan had to shore up their case and got creative. The Nevada Supreme Court handed the university the victory that the evidence was denying them.

It is noteworthy to explain that judges and justices are not fact-finders; disputed facts are within the province of the fact-finder (the jury). So even if the university had made the argument with supporting evidence that I had conflicts with other coaches, I had produced evidence that I had been praised for my interpersonal relationships. Only a jury could make the determination on such disputed facts. Also, at the summary judgment stage, the judge and justices were *required* to accept my evidence and any reasonable inferences drawn from it as true. Obviously they did not do that. This example shows that they were violating the very laws they were elected to uphold.

*   *   *

UNR conceded that it had unsuccessfully attempted to submit fabricated Nevada and ASU personnel files to the district court; the most egregious act of all in an employment case. The Supreme Court looked the other way. They decided in favor of the side of lies and deception and ignored the facts and evidence. If the university had any case whatsoever against me, why would they have gone to such illegal – and outright criminal – lengths and risk so much?

*   *   *

Running out of imaginative rationales to cover for UNR's inadequate defense, the justices wiped out nine of the claims with just two simple sentences.

We have considered the other claims raised by Patraw. We conclude they lack merit.

Within these nine claims were the claims that Judge Flanagan belatedly threw out without notice to me in his amended May 18th order of dismissal. This action by Judge Flanagan guaranteed their reversal in every court in every state in the United States. Unable to come up with any written rationale to support the misconduct by Judge Flanagan and the university administration, the justices whitewashed the claims in two sentences.

It was clear throughout that the order was not based on the case record. And as demonstrated by their own gaffes – in missing Judge Flanagan's recusal and in issuing an order that contradicted their own previous order – they did not review the record at all. I was deliberately denied my right to be heard by five justices of the Nevada Supreme Court. A judgment is void if its entry failed to comply with due process. *Mainor v. Nault*, 101 P.3d 308 Nev. (2004).

* * *

Even though the US Supreme Court hears very few petitions that come before them, in 2012 we decided to petition the court despite the odds. According to their own published statistics, the US Supreme Court receives approximately 10,000 petitions per year and hears only 75-80 of them. I knew it was a long shot because my petition did not fall into the category of cases that they typically hear.

But I had to give it a shot because I was not a quitter, and held onto the sliver of hope that judicial corruption would be considered an issue of paramount importance to our US Supreme Court justices. Nevada citizens were not being afforded equal protection of the laws, a violation of the Fourteenth Amendment of the US Constitution.

What I hoped would help my chances of being heard was that judicial corruption was an ongoing issue in the state of Nevada. This was an issue much broader than my own. In fact, in April 2012 another Nevada case was pending before the US Supreme Court in which the plaintiff had also accused the Nevada Supreme Court justices of fabricating the record.

In *Schulz Partners, LLC v. Zephyr Cove Property Owners Association, Inc*, the questions presented to the US Supreme Court read, in part:

Whether intentionally appearing, demonstrably false factual matters drafted by an officer of the Nevada Supreme Court . . . were so egregious as to be a fraud on the court and whether the resulting decision should be adjudged null and void on due process grounds.

Whether, under any circumstance, the finality of a judgment obtained by fraud is more important than due process rights emanating from the Due Process Clauses or a court's obligation to fairly decide cases.

The US Supreme Court had declined to hear that case. But we cited *Schultz* in my October 2012 petition, arguing that judicial fraud in the state of Nevada was an ongoing issue and implored them to intervene on behalf of all Nevada citizens who were victims or potential victims of this judicial corruption. But my petition was not heard and it seemed that perjury, lies and fraud would continue to be legal vices in the state of Nevada.

The flagrant abuse of the administration of justice is not what we learn growing up in America. My social studies teachers skipped over the chapter on judicial corruption; instead we were taught about a system of checks and balances and how Lady Justice ruled blindly and without prejudice. Our justice system is supposed to stand for something. But what I – and so many other Nevada citizens – encountered can only be described as a corrupt system that favors legal insiders and those with political juice.

As John C. Kirkland, an attorney from Santa Monica, California, said:

> I don't think what goes on in Nevada bears any resemblance to a justice system. It's an old-boy network. It's not a legal system *(Goodman and Rempel)*.

CHAPTER 18

Sunlight

"Each time a man stands up for an ideal, or acts to improve the lot of others, or strikes out against injustice, he sends forth a tiny ripple of hope."

~ Robert F. Kennedy

Back in 2006, while I was leading the Nevada soccer team to the conference championship, Rich, Lane and Hussein had flown to Las Vegas to meet with the FBI about widespread corruption on the University of Nevada, Reno campus. During this visit, they met with two FBI intake agents for over six hours while presenting evidence of retaliation, federal witness intimidation, witness tampering, manufacturing evidence, perjury, embezzlement, misuse of Federal funds and money laundering.

The agents indicated that they were very appreciative of their efforts and felt that some very important matters had been brought forward. There were several follow-up phone calls over the next few months with an Assistant Special Agent-in-Charge. Eventually the ASAC called with an update saying that he had to get the US Attorney's Office to agree to prosecute the case before the FBI would commit to carrying out the investigation. This was a case that would require a lot of resources and if the US Attorney would not prosecute, the investigation could not go forward. Subsequently, the US Attorney's Office informed the agents that they would not prosecute this case. The FBI's hands were tied. The ASAC did leave the door open by encouraging Rich, Lane and Hussein to continue to bring forth more information, which could perhaps convince the US Attorney to eventually agree to prosecute. He also recommended that they bring the state law violations to the attention of the Nevada Attorney General (NAG). But they were reluctant to do so because they knew that the UNR General Counsel's Office had close ties with the NAG's Office.

I had met with Rich, Lane and Hussein at our favorite watering hole – Starbucks – when they shared this information with me about their meeting with the FBI. They felt it was time to revive those efforts, and also decided to contact the NAG's Office. Together we recognized the damage and destruction that the university administration was doing to employees, students, and even to animals at the taxpayers' expense. The administration had no conscience and showed no signs of developing one.

In April of 2008, Rich had scheduled a meeting in Reno with NAG Catherine Cortez Masto. He asked us to join him. Assistant Attorney General Keith Munroe was also present and was visibly uncomfortable with us. NAG Masto listened to our presentation and then asked if we were also going to head to Las Vegas with our concerns. Reading between the lines, she was asking if we planned to bring this complaint to the attention of the US Attorney and FBI. The question was curious and the answer should not have mattered to her.

Heading into this meeting with NAG Masto, we were well aware that the entire legal team at UNR including Mary Dugan, Charles Hilsabeck, Frank Roberts, and Joe Ward had all been hired right out of the AG's Office. They were all buddies and former colleagues of Masto's staff. We knew there was an obvious conflict but we had no choice. This was the top cop in the state and her office was charged with investigating state law violations.

The AG's civil division also assists in the defense of UNR administrators and pays for private law firms to assist UNR legal counsel when necessary. The law firm, McDonald Carano Wilson LLP (MCW), and Reno Attorney Kent Robison were both hired by the NAG as defense counsel on UNR cases. MCW lawyers, Robison, and the entire UNR legal team were deeply implicated in the criminal complaint that we presented to NAG Masto. So as we met with her, we knew that we were asking that her criminal division keep these matters separate from her civil division. Masto acknowledged the absurd conflict when she stated that she was currently defending individuals we were trying to bring charges against.

Welcome to Nevada.

We suspected that the AG would whitewash the investigation. But as the FBI had informed Rich, Lane and Hussein, state law violations were under the authority of the NAG. AG investigator Wayne Fazzino was assigned to the case. Despite his assertions early on that he would meet with us, he never did. Instead he began to threaten and intimidate us telling us that we should withdraw the complaint. His so-called investigation consisted of making calls to his pals at the university and taking their word that there was no wrongdoing. Fazzino failed to address at least 135 of the allegations in his final report. Rich contacted Masto repeatedly about concerns with their shoddy investigation. She never responded.

On May 1, 2008, a couple of weeks after we met with the NAG, we flew to Las Vegas and met with Russell Marsh, Chief Criminal Division and Assistant US Attorney, State of Nevada, to provide his office with a copy of the complaint. We were seeking US Attorney Gregory Brower's commitment to prosecute the principals following an investigation by the FBI. It was immediately clear that the US Attorney's Office had been tipped off by the NAG because Marsh had detailed knowledge of the complaints lodged by Dr. Schweickert and Dr. Hussein.

After much hesitation, which heightened our suspicions, Marsh agreed to review our information and said that he would meet with us in Reno later in May 2008. Since this initial meeting in Las Vegas on May 1, 2008, to the present time, we have had no communication from the Nevada US Attorney's Office. Seems he forgot to get back to us.

In September 2008, in a troubling discovery, Hussein uncovered one of Attorney Kent Robison's billing records. This record, dated May 9, 2008, one week after our meeting with the Assistant US Attorney, indicated that the US Attorney's Office had sent a report detailing our complaint and evidence TO the university legal team. Instead of working with the FBI to investigate and prosecute, the US Attorney's Office leaked the evidence to the accused. The US Attorney had violated the public trust.

One wonders how Eric Holder, sworn in as Attorney General of the United States in 2009, would have felt about this action by the US Attorney's Office in Nevada:

Your job as assistant US attorneys is not to convict people; your job is not to win cases. Your job is to do justice. Your job is in every case, every decision that you make, to do the right thing. Anybody who asks you to do something other than that is to be ignored.

US Attorney Brower had previously worked in private practice with Mary Dugan, UNR's General Counsel. This explains why his office leaked evidence to his former colleague instead of supporting an FBI investigation of the complaint. In 2009, Brower was replaced by Daniel Bogden, who most recently had been employed by MCW. MCW attorneys were implicated in the complaint to the US Attorney's Office. Further, Bogden was recommended for US Attorney by Senate Majority Leader Harry Reid, whose son, Leif, was also implicated in the complaint.

Was there a pattern? The US Attorney's Office had also been accused of leaking information to individuals under investigation in the massive corruption scandal in Las Vegas that the late David Amesbury was involved in – this was detailed in Chapter 5. The US Justice Department lawyers in Washington D.C. have taken over that case from Nevada's US Attorney's Office. It seems that we weren't the only ones who didn't trust Nevada law enforcement. Bogden's office is also currently under congressional scrutiny for its refusal to prosecute cases generated by agents with the Bureau of Alcohol, Tobacco, Firearms, and Explosives (ATF). His office dismissed several ATF cases involving people who had been indicted by federal grand juries on illegal weapons and drug charges. His prosecutors turned away other cases involving violent criminals, allowing them to walk free and face no charges.

Again, welcome to lawless Nevada.

Back at the coffee shop, skeptical of the NAG and US Attorney offices, Rich Schweickert floated the idea of convening a grand jury investigation of UNR officials. He had done some research and found that Nevada was one of only a handful of states that allowed private citizens to petition the court for a grand jury investigation of public officials. Something, someone, anyone had to stop this den of crime hidden under the name of a university.

On May 14, 2008, two months after all of the fraud was exposed in my reinstatement case – and before we knew how perverse the judicial system in Nevada was – Rich, Lane and I petitioned the District Court for a grand jury investigation of UNR officials. A Grand Jury consists of citizens empanelled by the courts to decide whether someone should be charged (indicted) with a serious crime. The process under Nevada law was simple and by all outward appearances required very little work on our part. But we should have known that nothing involving UNR was ever easy.

While the statute requires a judge to act on the petition within five days, our petition sat nearly idle in the system for 16 months before it was heard. Six of the eight judges in the district court – including Judge Flanagan – recused themselves, one after the other, due to admitted conflicts of interest with the university and its officials. What were the odds that that seventy-five percent of the state judges would have conflicts with one organization? Those were odds that probably no self-respecting bookie would entertain.

The law in Nevada declares that judges have a duty to sit on all cases before them unless there is a conflict of interest. While they followed that rule and recused themselves in this high profile grand jury petition, in the past all of these same judges had accepted civil cases where UNR was the defendant. And in each of these cases, the judge in question had ruled in favor of UNR and threw the plaintiff's case out. I'd say the decks were stacked in favor of the university. The duplicity of their non-recusals in the civil cases was shamefully obvious. When we presented our grand jury petition, the judges didn't want to touch it with a ten-foot pole, perhaps even out of fear that their own name would surface amongst the evidence. Their cozy relationships with UNR demonstrated the incestuous entanglements between the courts and the university. The two entities nearly co-existed as one within the Nevada judicial system. The National Judicial College, in which many of the state judges participate annually, is even located on the UNR campus.

One of these judges, Janet Berry, initially accepted the grand jury petition and immediately threw it out based on unfounded language that she evoked. We appealed to the Nevada Supreme Court for a reversal of that decision. The petition was remanded back to Judge Berry with instructions to carry out her responsibilities on our behalf. The language Judge Berry used even befuddled the Nevada Supreme Court justices. Their response to our appeal read in part:

The district court . . . assigns language to that provision that is not found in the statute. We are at a loss as to the source of the language the district court assigns to NRS 172.175 . . . Therefore, we conclude that the district court manifestly abused its discretion . . .

Accordingly, we ORDER the petition GRANTED IN PART AND DIRECT THE CLERK OF THIS COURT TO ISSUE A WRIT OF MANDAMUS instructing the district court to conduct an evidentiary hearing and consider petitioners' petition in light of the proper construction of NRS 172.175 and make findings of fact in support or rejection of impaneling a grand jury to investigate petitioners' allegations of corruption against UNR officials.

This was a curious order by the Nevada Supreme Court as the statute said the judge was to decide based on the allegations in the written petition, not based on a presentation of the evidence. We should not have been forced to overcome this extra hurdle. The Nevada Supreme Court had the authority under the statute to send it directly to the Grand Jury when we appealed it. But they clearly were not willing to take on that responsibility and instead sent it back to the district court.

After the petition was sent back to Judge Berry, we asked her to disclose any conflicts of interest she had with the university and its officials. Her dismissal of the complaint had raised red flags. Among several other conflicts, she noted that her husband was "a very large donor" to the University of Nevada athletic department. We asked that she remove herself from the matter and she complied. It seemed that Judge Berry's conflicts of interest with the university got in the way of an honest order by this sitting judge in Reno, Nevada. The petition was moved into Judge Connie Steinheimer's courtroom. The evidentiary hearing would be held in an open courtroom and anyone, including the potential defendants and their attorneys, could attend the proceeding as spectators.

Based on what was indisputably an unusually high rate of recusals, we knew that we were up against a challenge that was far beyond just a simple case of presenting our evidence and convincing a judge that there was cause for a grand jury criminal referral. We weren't naïve. What were the chances that Judge Connie Steinheimer, who finally took on our petition, had no connections with UNR, or with the other judges who were conflicted with UNR, or with the university lawyers or the private lawyers that the university had hired? I'd say most bookmakers wouldn't take that bet either. But we had no choice and had to move forward and hope for the best.

This was a tough personal decision for me. I don't like labels for myself or for others. I am not a whistle blower. I hate that term. But what I am is a coach, a leader, a mentor and an honest person who not only works hard but relishes it. I'll take those labels. What made my decision to embark on this strange and unknown journey easier was the support I received from my family and friends, of course, and from my new friends – Drs. Schweickert and Hussein and police officer Lane Grow – who represented the full spectrum of honest citizens and employees who had suffered at the hands of criminals at the University of Nevada. But I wouldn't be taking one for the team. I was part of the team – a team that cared about the university and its great employees and its students – present and future.

As US Supreme Court Justice Louis Brandeis once famously said, "Sunlight is said to be the best of disinfectants." We hoped he was right and that our case would allow the sunlight to break through and expose the university administration for what it was.

We knew, of course, the best laid plans of mice and man . . . you know the rest. We weren't naïve and we knew that the university wouldn't just lie down for us. We recognized that we had obstacles and challenges to deal with, but we were determined. There is an innate sense of justice that man is born with. You can see it on the schoolyard playground with the tiniest of kids screaming that, "It's not fair!" when the other kids don't let him have a turn at bat or the chance to kick the soccer ball. Just like the little kid, we were screaming inside for justice and we wouldn't be satisfied until we got it. The university was treating its employees in a despicable, even illegal, manner and needed to be stopped. My desire to return to coaching had not diminished. It was my future. But my present was a fight for survival and justice . . . for me and for all who had suffered or would suffer in the future.

The filing of the grand jury petition set off an even greater series of vicious retaliations. They tried everything imaginable to knock me off my feet. But they didn't.

I'm still standing.

CHAPTER 19

Sealed Orders

"Everything was perfectly healthy and normal here in Denial Land."

~ Jim Butcher, Cold Days

As news got out that an evidentiary hearing was going to be held, we received several anonymous communications and phone calls from university insiders, current employees, who gave us some tips on specific documents that would help support our petition. Their desire to help us was heartening since it was obvious that we had many employees on our side. Their reluctance to speak out publicly was a reminder of the oppressive environment that was pervasive at the university, and that intimidation and the fear of retaliation was alive and well at the University of Nevada, Reno.

Working with Rich was like working with a lawyer. He was so proficient and adept in his role as spokesman and legal expert that if he hadn't chosen to become a geologist, he certainly would have had another profession waiting for him. Actually they could have used an attorney with his honesty and attention to detail in Reno, a town filled with corruption and a justice system that didn't live up to its name.

Learning that the district court was being forced to honor our petition and hold an evidentiary hearing, UNR tried several times to intervene but was repeatedly told that the university had no standing. University officials knew how dangerous my testimony was to Glick, Groth, Dugan and their private attorneys. Their goal was to stop me from testifying.

Revealing their desperation, the lawyers had Dugan's friend – Judge Patrick Flanagan – write up a void 15-day temporary restraining order against me conveniently interfering with the evidentiary hearing. As detailed in Chapter 15, Flanagan had lost jurisdiction to issue any orders in my case as of April 28, 2009 – the day his representation of his former client Craig Beattie was first at issue. This retaliatory order was fabricated by Judge Flanagan three months after his relationship with Dugan, Beattie and Reid had been exposed. Additionally, my case had left the jurisdiction of the district court because it was – at that time – on appeal to the Nevada Supreme Court. "We have no more right to decline the exercise of jurisdiction which is given, than to usurp that which is not given. The one or the other would be treason to the constitution." *United States v. Will*, 449 US 200 (1980). "A void judgment is one which has no legal force or effect whatever, it is an absolute nullity" (*Black's Law Dictionary*).

The order – as it was written – forbade me from speaking to Lane and Rich or to any other employee of the university; that would be thousands of citizens in small town of Reno, including many of my friends! The motivation of the lawyers – led by Dugan and Robison – was obvious, and the unconstitutionality of the order was so absurd that I actually had to chuckle. It may have been Nevada but last time I looked, Nevada was within the US borders and its people were protected by the US Constitution. I ignored the invalid order, as did Lane and Rich and even Judge Steinheimer.

In spite of the efforts to derail our petition, we at last got our evidentiary hearing on September 17 and 18, 2009, in Judge Steinheimer's court. Rich started off the hearing informing Judge Steinheimer that we would show during this two-day evidentiary hearing that the University of Nevada, Reno was a RICO operation. The Racketeering Influenced and Corrupt Organizations Act (RICO) is a group of federal laws that was passed by the United States Congress in 1970 that deals with organized racketeering activity. RICO law is focused on individuals or organizations involved in systematic and long-term illegal activities. I will take you inside the courtroom for a moment and let you hear it straight from Rich as he addressed Judge Steinheimer:

> UNR and the Nevada System of Higher Education have no rights in this hearing, . . . And, in fact, we believe there should be no concern whatsoever at UNR/NSHE if they have nothing to hide.

However, knowing that this matter is a petition between we citizens and this Court, UNR/NSHE has tried very hard to intervene for more than a year through various legal counsels: NSHE Chief Counsel Bart Patterson, UNR General Counsel Mary Dugan, Assistant General Counsels Frank Roberts and Charles Hilsabeck, and outside counsel Kent Robison.

There are at least six different attempts that are detailed on these slides. The first failed attempt was by Mr. Hilsabeck in June of '08. That was struck down by an order from Judge Berry . . ."NSHE is not properly named party to this matter, and any documents filed on its behalf will not be considered by the Court."

I'm not going to go through all of these in detail, but the second failed attempt was by Mr. Patterson, who is the chief legal counsel for the entire Nevada System of Higher Education.

On December 12th, essentially ignoring the earlier order by Judge Berry, he made a second attempt to intervene, and again Judge Berry stated clearly that NSHE has no statutory right to intervene. "Representatives of NSHE and UNR will not be permitted to participate in the evidentiary hearing ordered by the Supreme Court.

Petitioners had a July 1 phone case conference hearing with Your Honor, and on that date, July 1, the date of this hearing was set for September 17 and 18.

The very next day additional efforts to intervene began, the first one on July 2nd by Mary Dugan, UNR general counsel. She tried to tie the hands of one of our key witnesses by forcing him to be present at depositions scheduled for yesterday, today and tomorrow, knowing that he is to be a key witness at this evidentiary hearing. As the Court will learn this morning, this effort failed.

There was a fourth attempt directed at me, which I'll skip over right at the moment.

A fifth attempt by Mr. Robison on September 3rd, 2009 . . . . Mr. Robison persuaded District Court Judge Patrick Flanagan to restrict petitioner Patraw from any verbal or written contact with President Glick, some others, and any of his employees.

Both Judge Flanagan and Mr. Robison know the dates of this hearing and knowingly, we believe, violated the orders of Judge Berry and the Nevada Supreme Court.

This was calculated to prevent Ms. Patraw and me as co-petitioners from interaction and being able to stand here before you. Thankfully you have cleared that problem.

The most recent attempt was just a couple of days ago, September 10th. In another surprise hearing, NSHE and their attorneys, Hilsabeck and Dugan, persuaded a federal court judge to restrict a key witness from giving testimony at this hearing. They knew the dates and the purpose of this hearing when they filed those actions.

How dare we refer to the University of Nevada as a RICO operation? Let's look at the elements of racketeering that go on in RICO organizations as spelled out by the FBI. The middle part of this slide shows that racketeering activities typically include embezzlement, fraud, obstruction of justice, and money laundering.

UNR is a RICO operation, as we will maintain throughout this hearing.

Rich went on to present the majority of the evidence and questioned most of the witnesses. He laid out the university's violations of Federal RICO laws. He cited statutes and gave an overview of the criminal activities that he promised would be supported by evidence and witnesses over the course of the two-day hearing.

Dr. Hussein was the first witness and like all those who followed him was sworn in by the judge. He told his complicated and compelling story that encompassed everything from animal abuse to the long-term illegal, covert monitoring of his laboratory and office with surveillance cameras installed by the UNR police department. He and Rich presented evidence that legal counsel for UNR had manufactured evidence, tampered with witnesses, and embezzled funds. Hussein presented direct evidence that UNR attorney Charles Hilsabeck suborned perjury and that attorney Kent Robison was illegally billing the state for private services performed on behalf of UNR. Mary Lahren testified about the sexual harassment she endured from Dr. Karlin and the retaliation she suffered after she reported it. Rich described for the court how UNR was in violation of federal laws for covering up the charges that Mary Lahren had lodged against Karlin. He also detailed the intimate involvement of the Attorney General's Office in the criminal activity on the UNR campus.

Businessman Gregory MacRenaris testified about his knowledge of the illegal preferential treatment of vendors – in the millions of dollars – that was practiced by UNR. And Lane ended up the first day of our hearing testifying about his witnessing of widespread corruption at the UNRPD, including intimidation tactics, and was backed up by fellow officer Eric Hague. I spoke about numerous crimes that had been committed against me by Nevada Athletic Director Cary Groth, Executive Associate AD Cindy Fox and their band of attorneys, as well as by Judge Flanagan.

For the entirety of the hearing, Kent Robison, private attorney for UNR, Mary Dugan, UNR General Counsel, and William McGrath, an attorney at MCW, were present and listening to every word. Oh how the tables had turned. UNR's highly paid purveyors of deceit and lies were forced to listen to two straight days of unmitigated truth. I remember thinking that I hoped the evidence was making them realize that it was time to change their ways. But I was naïve to even entertain such thoughts. Glancing at the three of them now and then squirming uncomfortably in their chairs, I saw that they were staring down Judge Steinheimer as much as they were listening to the evidence. It was clear to everyone in the courtroom that they were acting in an intimidating manner toward the judge. They had chosen the three seats directly in the judge's sightline. The body language and stares and glares of these individuals, who Judge Steinheimer knew on a personal and professional basis, did not go unnoticed by her. In Nevada district court judges are elected. Attorneys fundraise for the judges, and Robison and McGrath possessed a great deal of financial and political clout over a judge's re-election campaign.

We had no problem with Judge Steinheimer during the evidentiary proceeding. She had no overt conflict of interest with UNR but a doubt lingered in my mind that she was completely impartial. Was she strong enough to stand up to the good-old-boys in small town Reno? I sensed that she wanted to hold a fair hearing and render an impartial judgment. But, it was obvious to everyone in attendance that the individuals facing potential criminal charges were doing their best to influence her decision.

Attorneys Robison and Dugan showed their true colors during the course of the hearing. They knew the bogus restraining order was invalid, which explained why they never had me served during its 15-day duration – which would render even a valid one void. In fact, Robison inadvertently admitted in open court that Judge Flanagan had no jurisdiction to issue it. However, during the middle of my presentation to the court, on the second day of the evidentiary hearing, a process server walked into the courtroom and served the already expired and void restraining order. Judge Steinheimer exploded! She literally shouted at Robison and informed us all that process service cannot happen in a courtroom . . ."EVER . . . NEVER!" So even this attempted and belated service of the expired order was invalid. The 65-year-old Robison swore to the judge that he wasn't behind this blatant retaliation. But in response to Robison's statement, the entire courtroom burst out laughing with a sarcastic edge that was unmistakable. I explained to the judge that the laughter was because Robison had been witnessed in the hallway setting this scheme up with the process server during the recess by nearly everyone present in her courtroom. Judge Steinheimer was livid. William McGrath of MCW walked out of the courtroom clearly embarrassed to be associated with Robison and Dugan. After admonishing Robison, the judge ordered her entire staff, including the bailiff into her chambers for an impromptu forty-minute meeting – probably to castigate them for losing control of the courtroom and allowing the process server to even step foot inside. The bailiff who provided security for the courtroom was called into that meeting leaving the courtroom unprotected and filled with two opposing sets of very angry people. It was inappropriate and an embarrassment to the judicial system. Although I was learning that the bar was set very low for the Nevada judicial system, it was, for all practical purposes, impervious to embarrassment.

Rich addressed the situation to Judge Steinheimer when she returned to the bench:

And now what the taxpayers just paid for is Mr. Robison having the audacity to serve this unconstitutional TRO to Ms. Patraw in the midst of her presentation of evidence in this hearing. And then I'm not sure if you're aware of this yet, then he gives an outright lie to the Court saying he doesn't know what's going on, even though he's just seen talking to the process server outside. This is a wonderful example for us of this sort of retaliation and intimidation, and here it took place in your courtroom, violated the sanctity of your courtroom.

Judge Flanagan had already revealed he had a dog in the race because he had recused himself from the grand jury petition and admitted he had several conflicts of interest with UNR. Flanagan had as much right to issue the restraining order as the card dealer in the casino one block from the courthouse. Knowing that Judge Flanagan acted outside his jurisdiction and would be vulnerable to being sued in his individual capacity for violating my constitutional rights, UNR lawyers never had me timely or properly served. Their shameless efforts were another disturbing attempt to intimidate me, and also to send a message that they have judges who are a part of their team.

*   *   *

At the conclusion of the second day of our hearing, Rich gave the closing argument:

We've seen examples of faculty, staff, coaches, police officers, and citizens who have evidence of criminal violations, and they've suffered massive retaliation at the hands of the whole University of Nevada, Reno retaliation apparatus that protects the upper-level administrators.

The retaliation apparatus involves the President's private police force, the UNRPD. It also involves the human resources and affirmative action offices.

Affirmative action is designed to protect the faculty, staff and students. But at UNR it's turned around and used as a tool for harassment by conducting secret investigations of honest employees.

You've seen evidence that the president's office and the attorneys working for the president's office have actually intimidated the local media to make sure that they're really just a mouthpiece for the university administration . . .

Other parts of the protection and retaliation apparatus are the general counsel's office. And that office is housed within the president's office. Therefore, everything that they do has the explicit recognition and approval of the upper administration.

What is all this trying to protect? It's trying to protect widespread abuses of the law involving financial crimes, athletic department crimes, police department crimes, EEO crimes, legal counsel crimes, and the whole UNR abuse of power.

UNR's message to faculty, staff, students and the public: If you challenge our power, we will threaten, intimidate, harass, demote, dismiss, sue and sanction you, and we'll get the taxpayers to pay for it.

We would have liked to have more witnesses come here, but we've been – well, number one, most of these witnesses are afraid to come forward because they know they'll be retaliated against. You don't see very many UNR people in this courtroom because they know General Counsel Mary Dugan is here most of the time taking names. Enough said on that.

I'm sure that when you first heard us say this or first read our documents you thought this was a pretty outrageous claim: UNR as a RICO operation. We submit to you that we have described and presented evidence that meets all 11 elements of the FBI RICO criteria.

Rich summarized everything succinctly and with great clarity. As I listened to his final argument, I felt sure we had proven everything we had set out to prove. Now it was up to the judge. We knew that it would be impossible for her to dismiss out of hand the majority of what we had presented. Judge Steinheimer had even commended our presentation of the evidence – stating that we were better than many attorneys who had appeared before her – a rather left-handed compliment all things considered.

In support of our efforts, the Nevada Association of Public Safety Officers (NAPSO) and the Nevada State Law Enforcement Officers' Association (NSLEOA) issued a joint press release on October 19, 2009, "Police Officers and the Community Fight Back Against Criminal Acts Committed by University of Nevada Reno Officials." Within the release, the American Civil Liberties Union (ACLU) and Reno Outreach for Animal Rights (ROAR) are both quoted expressing concerns about specific actions taken by university officials.

We were notified of her decision three months after the conclusion of the hearing. Curiously, UNR attorneys learned of the outcome before we did. The fact that the husband of an intern who worked for Steinheimer was an employee of Robison's law firm could have played a role.

The result of the two-day evidentiary hearing in Judge Steinheimer's court was a mixed one. She granted a grand jury investigation in part and denied it in part. But she filed her findings that she was sending to the grand jury under seal – so we were in the dark and so was the public. She based this action on her contention that grand jury investigations are always conducted in secrecy. While this is true, our proceeding was an evidentiary hearing; it was not a grand jury proceeding. It hadn't gotten to the grand jury yet! So, it was anyone's guess what happened. What did she refer to the grand jury? What action did the grand jury take if any? For all we knew, she could have sent a blank piece of paper over to them and thrown our evidence in the trash. We had also requested that the judge disqualify District Attorney Dick Gammick from the matter because he had refused to prosecute cases against UNR and had publicly declared that he was a huge fan of Wolf Pack athletics; but Steinheimer allowed him to stay on and he would be responsible for presenting the evidence to the grand jury.

The unsatisfactory outcome of this hearing was yet another example of the duplicitous nature of the judicial system that does not treat all cases and citizens the same. Around this same time, there was an evidentiary hearing in the same court for the notorious kidnapping and homicide of a young college coed. The results of that hearing were plastered all over the newspaper. But in our case, one involving the politically connected, our results were filed under seal, a clear departure from standard practice involving evidentiary hearings in Nevada. Judge Steinheimer's rationale for sealing the order was full of holes.

We didn't shrink from this latest assault on the taxpayers' rights or from what was a violation of fundamental fairness. We appealed to the Nevada Supreme Court again to have the results of the hearing unsealed. Coming as no surprise, in response to our appeal, Steinheimer requested assistance from the Attorney General's Office – one of the entities that Rich had implicated in the complaint before her! A good guess was that they would want to keep the matter sealed, too. This was a stunning conflict of interest and incredibly poor judgment by this sitting judge. We immediately demanded a recusal of the AG's Office, and in what must have been certain embarrassment, the AG's Office withdrew from the matter and referred it to a Las Vegas District Attorney's Office. But the district attorneys in Nevada are under the supervision of – you guessed it – the Attorney General.

The Nevada Supreme Court then stepped in and made an odd request. They said they would need to see the order that was filed under seal before they rendered a decision on our appeal. What was in the sealed order was not at issue. The question before them was whether or not Judge Steinheimer's rationale to file findings from an evidentiary hearing under seal was proper. After reviewing the sealed order, the Supreme Court unsurprisingly ruled that Judge Steinheimer's findings should stay sealed.

Rich, Lane and I finally had to face the reality that we were not going to get a fair hearing on the issues from either the Nevada Supreme Court or from the district court. By denying us the judge's conclusions, our hands were completely tied. In order to appeal what she denied to a higher court, we had to know what was in the sealed order! To this day we do not know the disposition of the petition. We have never learned what happened to the portion of our complaint that she allegedly granted. We came to believe that she probably didn't refer any of it. Our hopes that the judicial system would come through for the faculty, staff, students, and taxpayers were dashed.

This experience was nothing close to what I had been taught about American justice growing up in Minnesota's educational system. I would have never imagined that a group of citizens could present allegations of criminal wrongdoing supported by voluminous evidence and numerous witnesses and be virtually ignored by the judicial system.

Judge Steinheimer did not recuse herself because she said that she had no conflicts with the UNR. But for whatever reason, we were denied a fair hearing. We always suspected that Judge Steinheimer did have a conflict that she failed to declare. We did learn later that she had been the recipient of campaign funds from some of the lawyers implicated in the complaint.

If it was our right to have the hearing, didn't it follow that we had a right to learn what the result of that hearing was?! Apparently the "rights" of a citizen are treated selectively and on a case-by-case basis in the justice system in the city of Reno, in the county of Washoe, in the state of Nevada.

CHAPTER 20

The NCAA Investigation

"The NCAA has to establish their own rules and enforce their own rules."

~ Roger Goodell

In February 2008, the NCAA formally notified university officials that it had commenced an investigation into the University of Nevada athletic department that would be focused primarily on the allegations involving Golf Coach Rich Merritt. In what Groth apparently thought was a show of loyalty she made the following statement to the *Nevada Sagebrush*:

> Rich Merritt is still our golf coach. He paid his penalty, paid his dues and he served it. He's not getting fired (*Oxarart*).

But her loyalty was misplaced. Her statement was an act of defiance and an arrogant display of disregard for the NCAA and a blatant lack of support for her own university. She apparently was determined to retain Merritt on the university athletic staff no matter what she knew about his behavior and what the outcome of the NCAA investigation revealed.

But things got too hot as the investigation progressed and, feeling the pressure, Groth abandoned her vow to keep Merritt on and finally terminated him in May 2008. Still a favorite of Groth, Merritt was spared the damage of being publicly fired and was allowed to resign. Trying to soften Merritt's departure, several media outlets reported this comment attributed to university officials: "Nevada officials have insisted there's no connection between [Merritt's] resignation and the NCAA investigation."

However, Groth's own handwritten notes detailed her final meeting with Merritt at which she and Merritt discussed his numerous NCAA violations. Those notes included the following words: "Disappointing – need for a change. Not to be trusted. Sorry." Those were not words that conveyed the confidence of employer for employee.

Actually Merritt was given 24 hours to decide if he was going to resign or be terminated. The same day, Jean Perry, who oversaw university compliance, communicated with the NCAA enforcement staff, and promised to provide them with the press release announcing his departure the following day. Contrary to publicly released comments from Nevada athletic officials, Merritt's termination was directly related to the NCAA investigation.

*　　*　　*

In 2007, the university had conducted its own internal investigation of the NCAA violations alleged against Merritt. I had serious doubts about the legitimacy of their probe, especially as it related to the sports betting allegations. Taking a close look, the university did not use all possible resources and contacts it had at its disposal in pursuit of the facts surrounding the incidents in question.

Nevada was the only state that offered legalized sports wagering. Because of this, there had to be a heightened awareness by compliance officials at UNR and UNLV for possible NCAA violations. While sports betting is legal in Nevada, it is against NCAA rules for any student-athlete, coach, and athletic department employee to place bets on intercollegiate, amateur, and professional sports in which the NCAA conducts championships. This includes sports such as football, basketball, baseball, hockey, soccer, tennis, and golf. The use of insider knowledge and the opportunity to solicit student-athletes to partake in a point shaving scheme are of utmost concern to the NCAA. Point shaving compromises the outcome of games and is a federal crime.

Sandie Niedergall, Director of Compliance, made the comment that sports betting "went against everything that our department and NCAA represent." Of course, I was in agreement and that notion was what compelled me to report his illegitimate betting practices and other

NCAA violations in the first place. Jean Perry claimed that the school's investigation into the sports betting allegations was thorough. However, she failed to tap her local casino contacts in the probe, which would seem the most logical route to take to get to the bottom of an allegation of illegal betting. A review of the university's records into the investigation of Merritt revealed that they never accessed his university computer – including his Internet activity and UNR email account – or his credit card and checking accounts. As an employee working under the NCAA's governing rules, he would have been obligated to grant the school access to all of this information. The NCAA mandates that all of its athletes and employees fully cooperate in any university or NCAA probe. A failure to do so is a significant violation itself. The records produced by the university indicated that the school's investigation into the sports wagering allegations merely consisted of a handful of conversations with select individuals.

A university employee remarked that she had informed the administration that she had witnessed Merritt place bets in sports books on several occasions. But the employee said that there was no follow-up with her by anyone in the administration on what promised to be credible evidence of Merritt's sports wagering. The same witness also stated that Merritt had contacted her after Groth was first notified of his potential violations. Merritt informed the employee that Groth had met with him over coffee at Starbuck's and that Groth "said that after their meeting that she was going to write a letter to clear him." Merritt contacted this employee to let the individual know that despite what was seen and reported, he was going to be cleared of any wrongdoing. So the message to forget about what she had observed was crystal clear. Director of Compliance Sandie Niediergall said that Merritt gave her the same message immediately after his coffee date with Groth. Sandie said that he also informed her that "he had Groth's support." In response, Sandie sent an email to Groth just after Merritt stopped by her office:

From: Sandra L Niedergall
Sent: Friday, June 29, 2007 10:17 AM
To: Cary Groth
Cc: Cindy Fox
Subject: Richard Merritt

. . . [Coach Merritt] met with me and gave me a review of your talk. He also stated that a summary of your conversation would be forward to me by Monday with your analysis and comment . . . . I would like to gather all documentation as soon as possible so that this matter can be resolved quickly . . . .

Sandra L. Niedergall

Groth did not deny the contents of Sandie's email, rather six days later she simply wrote back and said "thank you Sandie." It apparently didn't matter to Groth if Merritt was putting the university at risk by placing illegal bets, a violation which had a commensurate punishment of termination. Rather, Groth's paramount concern appeared to be clearing him.

*   *   *

In March 2010, upon completion of its investigation, the NCAA sanctioned the University of Nevada and placed it on probation for three years for major violations committed by Merritt while overseeing both the men's and women's golf programs. Merritt was given a two-year show-cause penalty for his commission of several NCAA rules violations, including unethical conduct. The show-cause penalty essentially restricted any NCAA member institution from hiring him for the duration of the penalty. According to the NCAA, Merritt refused to cooperate on the portion of their investigation that focused on the charges that he had engaged in sports betting. He also provided false and misleading information to the NCAA. The following is a direct quote from NCAA findings in the Merritt investigation:

Several individuals . . . expressed their belief that [Merritt] wagered on sporting events. In an effort to confirm or repudiate this information, the enforcement staff requested access to the coach's financial records. Although [Merritt] provided access to his joint checking account, which showed a significant number of transactions at casinos in Reno and Las Vegas, he refused the enforcement staff's request for access to his credit card accounts *(NCAA)*.

Pursuant to NCAA Bylaw 10.1(d), individuals who "knowingly furnish the NCAA or the individual's institution false or misleading information concerning the individual's involvement in or knowledge of matters relevant to a possible violation of an NCAA regulation" will be charged with unethical conduct. Coaches and administrators rarely retain their jobs if they are found to be guilty by the NCAA of this violation. Student-athletes also face severe consequences for the same conduct. There are many recent and high profile examples.

In December 2011, Ohio State football coach Jim Tressel was given a five-year show-cause penalty. The NCAA made the following conclusion about the incident:

> Of great concern to the committee was the fact that the former head coach became aware of these violations and decided not to report the violations to institutional officials, the Big Ten Conference or the NCAA . . . . [He] falsely attested that he reported to the institution 'any knowledge of NCAA violations' . . . The former head coach's failure to report this information violated NCAA ethical conduct legislation *(NCAA)*.

In August 2011, University of Tennessee men's basketball coach Bruce Pearl was given a three-year show-cause penalty.

> The most serious allegations in this case involved [his] conduct in the commission of violations, the provision of false and misleading information about them, and the inducement of others to do the same *(NCAA)*.

In October 2009, Oklahoma State football player Dez Bryant was ruled ineligible for the final ten games of his junior season for lying to the NCAA about a potential NCAA violation. It turned out that the potential violation that the All-American wide receiver lied about wasn't a violation after all. But he was still punished for being untruthful to the NCAA investigators *(Watkins)*.

In December 2012, Texas Longhorn basketball player Myck Kabongo was suspended by the NCAA for the entire 2012-13 season; his suspension was later reduced to 23 games. He was found to have accepted inappropriate gifts and had provided false and misleading information to the NCAA *(Katz)*.

In general, the NCAA was proud of its equal treatment of those institutions and individuals involved in college sports. To underscore their unbiased image, in November 2009, NCAA spokesperson Stacey Osburn issued a written statement emphasizing that NCAA rules are applied equally to all individuals regardless of national prominence or level of athletic ability.

Our members have clearly spoken on the importance of honesty in athletics and expect all student-athletes and administrators to follow the principals of ethical conduct *(Watkins)*.

Considering all the foregoing examples – and there have been many more such cases over the years – I was, of course, at a loss as to why the NCAA didn't charge Groth with unethical conduct when she lied to its investigators about her concealment of allegations of NCAA violations in the Nevada men's basketball program. As detailed in Chapter 10, Groth had told the NCAA investigators that she had discussed allegations that were brought to her attention with Dr. Chris Exline. But Exline had passed away two months before she was even aware of the allegations. The NCAA investigators knew this was not an innocent mistake by Groth. They had been informed prior to their interview with Groth, that she had proffered the same lies twice during under-oath depositions.

But Groth kept digging herself in deeper and deeper with her aversion to the truth. My legal team had not initially informed Groth that we were aware of her blatant lies. But after several months into the process, we finally addressed it in a brief to the court. At that point both she and Team Dugan knew she was in trouble with the NCAA. So they went to work on a new cover-up to cover up the original cover-up – the Dr. Exline lie. Because the NCAA investigation was still ongoing, Groth sent an affidavit to the NCAA in an attempt to do some damage control. Groth's new story was that she was "confused." According to Groth, there had been another report of violations in the men's basketball program – an anonymous report – that she had spoken to Exline about. She said that she had mixed up the two reports in her interview with the NCAA.

It was a weak attempt at recovery and we did not buy it for one second. So Jeff went to work, deposing Groth about her affidavit and its accompanying story.

Q   You – as I understand those affidavits, your explanation is that you mixed it up with an anonymous complaint; is that correct?

A   That is correct.

Q   Does that refresh your recollection as to what time frame we're looking at here?

A   It does.

Q   And when would that be?

A   *In spring of '06, early spring.*

Q   Okay. And what was the nature of the anonymous complaint that you talked to Dr. Exline about?

A   It had to do with men's basketball and the compliance of men's basketball, NCAA rules.

Q   Did that ever go beyond the campus in terms of investigation?

A   *Dr. Exline investigated that.*

Q   That's as far as it went?

A   I can't answer that question. I don't know.

Q   You don't know. What was the allegation?

A   *The allegation was [sic] involved student athletes, men's basketball players studying in the men's basketball office.*

But Perry replaced Exline on January 1, 2006. Exline was not involved with NCAA compliance at Nevada in the *Spring of 2006*. Her "confusion" was not an excuse. It was her duty to report any allegation of misconduct to compliance no matter who was in charge of the office at the time. Both Jean Perry and Sandie Niedergall – the two compliance officials who were in place in 2006 – had previously testified that they had not been made aware of any allegations of violations in the men's basketball program by Groth. Therefore, Groth utterly failed in her responsibility to make the appropriate report. She wasn't "confused" about the reports – she didn't report them to anyone. Groth's never-ending lies brought Sandie back to the table . . . under oath. Sandie had been the Director of Compliance for Groth's entire Nevada tenure. She was asked about Groth's *anonymous complaint regarding players studying in the men's basketball office*:

Q Did you ever investigate allegations that student athletes on the men's basketball program were being allowed to study in the coach's office?

A No

Jean Perry had previously explained how investigations work at Nevada:

Q And can you explain the chain – how it works the – for investigating these violations? Where it starts, who it goes to next, et cetera?

A It can start anywhere. Any time that we are made aware of potential violations, we investigate it, and including anonymous allegations. It's our job to try to get to the bottom of anything – that's alleged. When is an allegation, Sandra Niedergall does the investigation. She has total authority to consult with whoever she needs and wants to consult with. We ask her to keep very extensive records . . .

But, to the surprise of no one, there were no records of this "anonymous" report.

The NCAA was aware that Groth proffered new lies to them in her affidavit to cover her old lies from her interview. She was just as inept at her cover-ups as she was at her job. Inexplicably, the NCAA did not charge Groth with unethical conduct for providing false and misleading information on either occasion. Clearly the rules had not been "applied equally to all individuals" as Stacey Osburn had publicly declared. The allegations – which were willful recruiting violations by the men's basketball staff – were supported by documentation, including phone records, bank records, and airline tickets. Yet both Groth and the basketball staff were let off the hook by the NCAA's enforcement staff.

In 2013, University of Miami President, Donna E. Shalala, released a statement regarding the NCAA enforcement staff's conduct in the recent investigation of her school:

Sadly the NCAA has not lived up to their own core principles . . . .
Regardless of where blame lies internally with the NCAA, even one

individual, one act, one instance of malfeasance both taints the entire process and breaches the public's trust.

The NCAA demands full compliance and truthfulness of its members in enforcement cases. All employees are obligated to cooperate fully and truthfully with all NCAA inquiries. I was stunned and disappointed that the NCAA enforcement staff – led by David Price, the NCAA's vice president for enforcement at that time – covered up Groth's misconduct. Miami President Shalala's statement is certainly applicable to Price's handling of the University of Nevada case.

Price also looked the other way when Perry with the assistance of Groth and Cindy Fox fabricated the NCAA reports that pertained to me. While the NCAA did not charge me with any violations, they did not sanction the trio of administrators for fabricating NCAA reports to cover up their own misconduct. Price was aware that both Groth and the university had admitted to retaliating against me for reporting Merritt's violations, which is also in violation of NCAA principles. And, finally, Price and his staff knew that Nettie, at the behest of the administration, was soliciting student-athletes to write false complaints. Certainly this was not an example of the student-athlete experience that the NCAA promoted in its stated mission. David Price failed to take any action; rather, he allowed Groth and company to inappropriately use his revered organization as a tool of retaliation with impunity.

David Price also steered clear of a thorough investigation into allegations of academic fraud in the men's basketball program. A university employee reported that she had witnessed it herself. There were several other individuals who had reported similar allegations of academic anomalies surrounding the basketball program. The initial witness was so concerned about retaliation by the university that she chose to meet with the NCAA investigators off-campus and without the university's knowledge. The NCAA investigators arranged the meeting and assured her of confidentiality. But later, Cindy Fox informed the employee that the athletic department had been notified that she had met with NCAA officials. That employee left the university shortly thereafter.

The handling of Groth and the Nevada investigation by David Price and the NCAA could be characterized at its best as perfunctory and at its worst as biased. But the odds would be that those who suffered punishment for their violations – Tressel, Pearl, Bryant, and Kabongo among many others – would have a stronger choice of words for this glaring disparity. Tressel and Pearl were terminated from their multi-million dollar coaching jobs after being charged by the NCAA for providing false and misleading information. Bryant and Kabongo each lost nearly an entire season of eligibility. But the athletic director at Nevada – the position that should be held to the highest standard – got away with lying, not once but twice, to the NCAA. Ironically, in his letter of suspension, Groth had admonished Merritt for providing "false and misleading information concerning [his] violations." The NCAA does not typically have a soft spot for athletic directors. In 2011, the then-AD at the University of Central Florida resigned after being charged with providing false or misleading information to the NCAA. Tribble also was given a three-year show-cause penalty.

So this begs the question – why did David Price and his staff cover up so much at Nevada?

*   *   *

On November 15, 2007, one week after the NCAA enforcement staff had quietly begun its investigation of Nevada, the university held a grand opening ceremony for its brand new "Joe Crowley Student Union." Joe Crowley was the former university president and was also a former president of the NCAA. One of the guests at this grand opening for the new union in Crowley's honor was Myles Brand, President of the NCAA from 2002-2009 – Myles passed away in September 2009. He had flown from Indianapolis to Reno to celebrate the grand opening with Crowley. Myles also appeared to have had a strong relationship with Groth, as evidenced by chummy handwritten notes such as "call Myles" and "Myles' birthday" on her calendar. Groth and Crowley also had a tight relationship by all appearances. Crowley was a constant presence in the stands on campus at both men's and women's sporting events and Groth was usually sitting right there next to him.

Jeff and I had our suspicions about these seemingly over-friendly relationships so we asked UNR to produce all emails between Crowley and NCAA officials. Crowley, while retired from the President's office at the time, still taught classes, had an office on campus, and used his university email account. So UNR was required under the Nevada's open records act to produce them. But Dugan refused to produce what she said were "dozens" of emails between Joe Crowley and the NCAA. If the emails would clear him and there was no mischief going on why not produce them?

I liked Joe Crowley. He was a huge supporter of athletics at Nevada and a big supporter of mine when I worked there, having served as the UNR President during part of my tenure:

Terri . . . I am so pleased the soccer program has enjoyed such success. I know that the major reason for that success is, of course, the coach. Congratulations to you on a great job in building the program and in particular for the conference championship and the NCAA tournament this year. That's a remarkable accomplishment! . . .

Joe Crowley

Joe also spoke to me several times shortly after I left the university. He attempted to mediate the situation between myself and the university before any damage was caused to either side. That was laudable of Joe but if Joe Crowley interfered with the NCAA investigation to protect Groth, he not only undermined the university he betrayed the student-athletes in the process. A release of all emails between Crowley and the NCAA would have shined light on the truth no matter what it was.

The longer the university hung onto Groth and covered up her wrongdoing, the more dire the situation grew for the athletic department. In 2010, Nevada was placed on NCAA probation and the golf programs suffered scholarship losses as part of the sanction. In 2011-12, Nevada finished at the bottom of the conference in on-field performance across all sports. The soccer program has not had a winning season since my last day there. And, the athletic department, in 2012-13, boasted the smallest operating budget in its conference.

Did Myles Brand pressure David Price into violating the very rules he was paid to enforce? Or did David Price alone make the inexplicable decision not to punish Groth et al. for what were indisputable violations involving the NCAA's most sacred principles of ethical conduct?

Nevada is the second institution that landed on NCAA probation under Groth's leadership. Groth's former institution – Northern Illinois University – where she had previously served as AD was also sanctioned by the NCAA for major violations committed during her tenure there. The person most implicated at NIU in that case was later hired by Groth at Nevada.

It is clear that Groth and I had different value systems when it came to NCAA compliance and protecting the integrity of the institution. But what does it say about an AD who has so little regard, not only for her successful coach, but, more importantly, for the student-athletes?

Groth destroyed the soccer team's chances for more championships at the very pinnacle of their college careers. The college years pass by quickly. Student-athletes don't get a Mulligan on those fleeting seasons of college sports.

CHAPTER 21

The Media

"When did fact checking and journalism go their separate ways?"

~ Jon Stewart

If you followed my story you are probably thinking that the evidence I have shared with you in this book bears little resemblance to what you read in the media.

This disparity was no accident. It was by design . . . the university's design. The president's office and the attorneys working for the administration – Dugan and Robison – intimidated and manipulated the local media to make sure that they were just a mouthpiece for the university administration. The truth was clearly irrelevant to some in the media whose entire careers hinge on the pursuit of truth. Not only did UNR officials spread lies through their puppets in the media, they warned their lackeys not to allow any stories that countered their fabricated version of reality to appear in their publications and be allowed to penetrate into the community consciousness.

Threatened with the promise that no interviews with Nevada's athletic department would be granted to them, these members of the media shrunk from their tasks, abandoned their reporter's soul and acquiesced to the wishes of Team Dugan. Bottom line, the crystal clear message sent to the local media from the powers that be at UNR was that they were to act as the university's marionettes. Further, if they wanted their "in" with the university, they dared not print any damaging information about university officials or events that took place at the university. Such damaging stories were to be avoided and squelched without fail.

As previously mentioned, UNR's outside attorney Kent Robison fraudulently billed the taxpayers $1,105 for a meeting with the *Reno Gazette Journal* editors and reporters – and several UNR administrators – in an effort to improve the image of the University of Nevada, Reno. Apparently it worked, because according to the meeting minutes for the AAUN – Nevada athletics' fundraising arm – Groth reported to her staff and top university donors that she had spoken to RGJ President Ted Power and that Power had assured her that "the RGJ has UNR's back." Having an organization's back is not the role of an honest and independent press. Power faced a dose of karma when he was later arrested for DUI and removed as President of the RGJ. Evidently, no one had his back.

Two members of the media – Martha Bellisle of the RGJ and Scott Sonner of the Associated Press – were the local reporters who covered my story as well as the NCAA investigation of Nevada. After observing their behavior and activities, I had no other option than to believe that they were part of the effort to cover up any and all bad news for the university and my story, the true account of events, was decidedly bad news for the university.

The university used Robison as their press liaison. Robison used the court as a way of protecting himself from defamation liability. Under the law, an individual cannot be held liable for defamation based on statements made in court. So any false statement that Robison made in open court or in court filings – that was subsequently published in the press – was protected. Bellisle was the only reporter who ever stepped foot in the courtroom in my case. She turned out to be the willing pawn of Robison and the university. Sonner's reports originated directly from UNR, replete with fabrications from their well-oiled spin machine.

Groth took advantage of a student reporter while also hiding behind the court-protected defamation laws. The student reporter called me one day several months after-the-fact to let me know that he had been used by Groth. He said that Groth had called him one day and told him to go to the court and read a filing by the university. The young reporter wrote a story without ever contacting me – or Jeff – or waiting for our response to their filing. What Groth knowingly sent him to review was a pile of fabricated documents submitted by the university lawyers. She used him to smear me in the press. He had called to apologize for being duped and expressed his wish that he had never written the story.

The first time I met Martha Bellisle of the RGJ was in the courtroom. It was nearly abandoned other than for a few people. There was a young woman front and center. I introduced myself to her and said that she looked familiar. She snapped at me, told me that I didn't know her and looked back at her papers completely ignoring me. She was telling the truth when she told me that I didn't know her but she was lying by omission because, of course, she knew who I was. I was taken aback by her hostile attitude.

When I learned that Bellisle was a reporter, it became apparent that she was there to cover my story. I couldn't help but wonder why she wouldn't want to converse with the principal in the story. I had my answer when Robison walked in. She immediately rose and greeted him. I was amazed as I watched him hand her a stack of documents and begin to underline certain lines that he presumably wanted her to report on. It could not have been more obvious. I, and a number of other people, later witnessed Bellisle huddled in the hallway giggling with Mary Dugan and Robison. She was blatant in her display of bias and in abandoning the ethical nature of her position. It is noteworthy that Bellisle was a graduate of UNR.

The Manti Te'o-Notre Dame-fake girlfriend scandal of 2012 taught us just how inaccurate and damaging news stories can be. In that case, a reporter wrote a story based on a single account but failed to do the basic fact-checking that any cub reporter would be expected to do. The story took off like quicksilver and soon media all over the world were reporting the same lies. Amazingly for months no one bothered to question the story. The lies became repeated as facts in thousands of news reports around the globe. The impact of such a lack of professionalism and an abandonment of ethics and responsibility can have damning and lasting impact on a person's life – impact that can be nearly impossible to reverse. In the case of Manti Te'o, perhaps the original reporter was drawn into the story and duped. That's not an excuse for a professional newsman but it's something that can happen. However, what's the excuse for the literally other hundreds of reporters who repeated the story like lemmings diving off the cliff?

In my story, Bellisle and Sonner were not innocently duped. These two reporters worked in cooperation with the university. Since there was no doubt that the university was trying to destroy me, the obvious conclusion was that these two reporters were helping them.

A mental tug-of-war was going on. With every negative article that appeared about me in the news, the university through the coordination with the local media was pushing me, trying to wear me down and get me to drop my case. But as it turned out, their strategy backfired on them. This tactic had exactly the reverse affect. It made it impossible for me to walk away. I could not let stand the lies they were spreading about me. They had smeared me so badly that I had no choice but to continue the fight to clear my name. I thought too much of my reputation and the stellar career that I enjoyed at the university to leave them behind, destroyed by ugly words and false accusations. I had to go forward. The university, in league with the local media, was out to ruin me. I had held onto the promise of justice; that a jury would hold the university and their morally deficient lawyers accountable for their actions.

Bellisle and Sonner's actions also contributed to my reasons for writing this book. They held in their hands the power of the press and wielded their pens to defame me and tarnish my reputation. But the pen has turned on them. I majored in journalism and understand the responsibility of objective reporting and journalistic integrity. Bellisle and Sonner failed on both fronts. They were offered a mission to destroy me and they didn't refuse it. Despite the fact that they didn't know me or my story, they followed their worst instincts and reported in a biased and negligent manner. They abandoned their principals to appease the lawyers and university that were opposing me. It's not only tragic that people have such little regard for a fellow human, it's astonishing that they have such little regard for their time-honored profession and on a grander scale their own morality.

I grew weary reading about my case in the local newspapers and in articles in the Associated Press. I lost count as to how many times I read, "In a whistleblower letter that Patraw sent last fall . . .", but I never sent a whistleblower letter! Then I would read what I allegedly said to someone when in reality I never said the words, never spoke to the person or even knew who he or she was. It was all lies and they were hurtful. And the situation was particularly frustrating because I had no way to battle the fabrications that were front-page news in the "Biggest Little City in the World." The press had been so cowered and intimidated by the university that they were afraid to print the truth. But just like in the Manti Te'o story, the untruths kept being reprinted in the press. Fact-checking apparently had become a thing of the past.

When working effectively and guided by morality, the media are essential parts of our culture. When they bring criminal activity to light, society-at-large is better for it. Without Sara Ganim, an ambitious and dedicated young reporter in Harrisburg Pennsylvania, Jerry Sandusky may never have been exposed for his crimes against young boys on Penn State University's campus. Ganim's courageous reporting on the Penn State scandal led to her recent hiring by CNN. She was rightly rewarded for her good work. Sadly, in some quarters good reporting is becoming the exception rather than the rule. While the short-term damage was painful to the community and university, society greatly benefited from Ganim's relentless and fearless reporting of Sandusky's crimes. No one in this country should be afraid to speak out – especially members of the press – it undermines the ideal upon which our nation was founded.

While both the fraud and the smear campaign that went on in my case occurred in other UNR cases, I paid a high price in the media because mine involved athletics. Throughout the entire experience, I felt like I was involved in the childhood game "Sticks and Stones" – *Sticks and Stones may break my bones but names will never hurt me.* The 12-year-old bully – disguised as Attorney Kent Robison – and his juvenile intimidation tactics through the media would not have been necessary if the university had an honest defense against my allegations. But as you have seen throughout this book, they never had a case; they knew they never had a chance in front of a jury of my peers. So the media tactic was employed to harass and defame me while destroying my reputation and polluting the jury pool. But their lies defined them, not me.

*   *   *

My first experience with the protection the local media afforded the university was approximately two months after I left the university. I was asked by Beryl Love, Executive Editor, and Lauren Gustus, Sports Editor, of the *Reno Gazette Journal* if I would meet with them and tell my story. They promised to report it exactly as I relayed it to them. After discussing it with my attorney, I decided in lieu of going through years of litigation, I would just tell my story and get out of town – redeem my reputation and make a clean break from the whole mess. However, just a couple of hours after meeting with the Reno Gazette representatives, I received a phone call from Lauren Gustus who was a relatively new editor with the paper. As soon as she began talking, I could sense that she was a bit shaken. She told me that Cary Groth knew that we had just met and had called the RGJ right after our meeting. Groth, who was apparently paranoid about what went on during the meeting, was obviously tracking my whereabouts. During our meeting, Beryl and Lauren had shared with me that UNR officials regularly threatened to remove any sources available to them if they reported the truth about the university administration. If the university had nothing to hide, they would not need to threaten the local media. A few days later, Lauren contacted me again to tell me that the paper decided against running the story. Her boss, Beryl Love, had caved to university pressure.

While the RGJ and other supporters of UNR wanted to believe that the local media were doing the university a favor, the reality is that media blackouts are some of the reasons why the institution, city, and state are last in nearly everything. The media's protection of inept and corrupt leaders in Nevada has contributed to the state being last in the nation in K-12 education according to a 2012 national study by *Kids Count*. The state has also faced the highest unemployment rate in the nation along with the highest foreclosure rate during the nation's recent economic crisis. In 2012, the Center for Public Integrity in Washington D.C. assigned to Nevada a D-minus grade, finding it low in transparency and vulnerable to political corruption. Not surprisingly, it received a failing grade in ethics enforcement. The University of Nevada athletic department has found itself at the absolute bottom of its conference in both on-field success and in overall operating budget. These poor results can at least be partially laid at the feet of the media; unscrupulous and incompetent leaders in government, judiciary and higher education are protected and go unexposed.

Outsiders who possessed leadership qualities, intelligence, and ethics were not welcome in Reno, Nevada. And, UNR administrators used the press to ruin anyone who dared to speak the truth to their avalanche of lies.

*　　*　　*

Athletic administrators at other institutions to whom I have spoken, expressed their astonishment at the level of protection afforded to UNR officials by the media. While many university officials admitted that the media are inherently biased in most small college towns, none felt that their institutions would be afforded the blatant protection that the Reno media provided to UNR.

I was speaking with an RGJ reporter – who, for his own protection, shall remain nameless – about my reinstatement case being remanded due to perjury, falsification of evidence, and concealment of documents by Groth et al. When I asked him why the RGJ continued to report that I had lost my reinstatement hearing when the newspaper was aware that the decision was remanded and no longer valid, he blurted out that "We are not allowed to report that Groth committed perjury." I was surprised by his candor but appreciated his honesty. Beryl Love controlled the editorial content of the RGJ so this directive undoubtedly came right from him.

Dr. Rich Schweickert had contacted Beryl Love several times to arrange a meeting to discuss the grand jury petition against UNR officials. Rich felt this was a huge public interest story that was deserving of significant media coverage. After all, it was the taxpaying citizens who were unknowingly footing the bill for the rampant retaliation on the UNR campus. Beryl refused to meet with him.

When the district court judge granted in part the grand jury investigation of UNR officials, AP writer, Scott Sonner, refused to report on this undeniably monumental story. Knowing that this story would have drawn the attention of the national media and the educational community, Sonner made sure that the local AP did not report it. The investigation of a university administration by a grand jury is virtually unheard of and would have grabbed national headlines. The RGJ buried the story – written by Bellisle – on page two despite the fact that it was obviously front-page material, especially in the hometown of the university under investigation. It was a disservice to the citizens of the community and to the students and faculty of UNR. Sonner also was a no-show at the two-day evidentiary hearing, which detailed the criminal activity that UNR officials were engaged in.

Sonner primarily covered the NCAA investigation of the University of Nevada. Notably missing from his reporting was the NCAA's most serious charges against Golf Coach Rich Merritt. It seems as though

Merritt's unethical conduct charge for refusing to cooperate in the sports betting probe and providing false and misleading information to the NCAA, along with his two-year show-cause penalty would have been of interest to readers. The NCAA confirmed that several witnesses provided statements confirming that Merritt had engaged in sports betting. Yet Sonner omitted this finding and wrote that "the NCAA found no evidence of sports betting by Merritt." The show-cause penalty essentially prohibited Merritt from coaching anywhere in the NCAA during the period of the penalty. The most significant charges issued by the NCAA – the unethical conduct charge and the show-cause penalty – also went unreported by the local media.

The RGJ published a scathing editorial which focused on a coach who had been fired at another university for providing false and misleading information to the NCAA. The editorial gave a sermon on the evils of lying. It preached that anyone who lied should not be allowed to hold a leadership position within the NCAA. Yet, aware that Rich Merritt and Cary Groth had both been guilty of lying – and in Groth's case, under oath – the RGJ went silent.

Despite their knowledge of the incident, the RGJ never reported that a Nevada head coach was arrested and convicted of a DUI after leaving the strip club *Fantasy Girls* just a few blocks from campus. Yet the same news organization reported without fail each time a student-athlete was arrested for the same violation.

Bellisle sat in regularly during my proceedings and saw first-hand the fraud, perjury and fabricated documents submitted by Groth, Robison and Dugan. But she ignored all of it and instead knowingly reported their lies. One day Bellisle called me for a quote for a story she was writing. I bluntly asked her if she was going to once again be the university's puppet in the writing of the article. She did not respond. A friend warned me to be careful. "She is going to be ruthless in this one," my friend said. Much to our surprise, the article she wrote was fair and balanced. But her newly found truth-in-reporting phase was short-lived.

Bellisle's and Sonner's reports were used by the local television stations and national media when they were sent out on the AP wire. KRNV Channel 4 in Reno is owned by Jim Rogers, the former Chancellor for the Nevada System of Higher Education. University athletic staff members have access to Channel 4's website passwords so they can access their files. Needless to say, this is an inappropriate arrangement and hardly representative of a pristine news organization who is in pursuit of facts.

I was a highly successful coach and ran a clean program, even winning a championship for the university. I repeatedly went out of my way to protect my employer from any liability. But not willing to face the reality that their sports program was in disarray, the university, in league with their lawyers and a willing and cooperative press, opted to orchestrate a smear campaign against me. And, when it came to their media mouthpiece Kent Robison discussing me, it would not be a stretch to say – "if his lips were moving, he was lying."

Accept no other definition of your life, accept only your own.

CHAPTER 22

Never-Ending Retaliation

"If right is right, it's right all the time, not just when its convenient."

~ Kathy Herman, The Right Call

I resisted writing this book despite the urging over the years by many to do so. It was not an appealing prospect to have to live through this nightmare again. But the never-ending and destructive actions of Groth finally gave me no choice. Books are written from inspiration or out of necessity. I was compelled to write this book because Groth's intrusion into my life perpetuated and still goes on to this day. I do not find joy in sharing the following account with you. But it is necessary to demonstrate the lengths that Groth et al. were willing to go to, and why I felt that I had no choice in writing this book.

Five years after I left the University of Nevada I lived several states away and had moved on with my life. But in the fall of 2012, eleven days after Groth publicly announced her "retirement", two anonymous emails were sent to my employer with provably false but highly inflammatory accusations about me. This was the catalyst, the final straw that forced me to write this book.

After reading the two emails I immediately knew who was behind the act of sabotage. I had been upfront with my employer so the organization was aware that I had been dealing with some very toxic people in Nevada.

Through a former colleague's observations of curious workplace behavior of both Groth and her hired blogger Ryan Jerz I learned that a blog had been created called blackpanter007.xanga.com. It has since been shut down by Xanga. The blog was created in my honor and was filled with many of the very same lies that were written in the emails to my employer. It was quite obvious that the same person(s) was behind both the blog and the emails.

Groth was notified through her attorney – John Arrascada – that I was aware of both the blog and the emails and that I knew that she was behind them. It is a crime in Minnesota – criminal stalking – to attempt to injure a person or their property through technology while falsely impersonating another. It was clear to me that this woman was never going to leave me alone so I brought this matter to the attention of law enforcement. Through that process I learned that the blog and the email account had both originated from a Charter Communications subscriber in Reno, Nevada. The Internet Protocol (IP) Address for the blog was identified as 71.84.127.17 on August 18, 2011, the day the blog was created. Arrascada was notified that this IP address had been assigned to the home of Groth's sister, Patricia (Groth) Newbrough, at that time and for a period of several months surrounding it. Groth admitted to using the Internet at her sister's Reno area home.

The two anonymous emails sent to my employer were signed by Sheryl Fall and Sheryl Hill – it seemed that she forgot which name she used in first email – and they were both sent from the same email address. The name "Carter Henry" was the pseudonym used to create the email account. "Carter Henry's" name was also found on the xanga blog.

While I cannot prove who created the blog or hit the send button on the emails – Groth, her sister, or some other family member who lived in the Newbrough home – it wouldn't take Sherlock Holmes to break that case. "Carter" was the last name of Groth's basketball coach and "Henry" was the name of Groth's dog. Additionally, the user identification (user name and password) was changed on the blog immediately after Groth was notified of my initial call to Arrascada.

Laying out the time line of this latest attempt to disrupt my life may clarify what had occurred. You can make your own conclusions.

On June 15, 2012, Groth emailed her subordinate and defamation ally Ryan Jerz. In her email to him she discussed her purported knowledge of my future employment plans. At that time, I had been gone from the university for five years and to this day I have never met Ryan Jerz. A review of Jerz and Groth's computer activity revealed that both had spent extensive time at work discussing and researching me. Clearly this was not a duty listed in their job descriptions.

On August 2, 2012, I received a not-so-nice email from Groth's brother John – who apparently lives in Indiana. He used his work email address and signed his own name. I have never met John Groth, but I assumed the email was spurred by Groth's upcoming retirement announcement.

On August 20, 2012, a flurry of defamatory statements about me was posted on the xanga blog.

On August 29, 2012, Groth's "retirement" was announced in the media. She was later forced to admit that she was not offered a contract extension to her expiring contract.

Five days later, on September 3, 2012, Groth sent another email to Ryan Jerz that said, "That site I was telling you about is blackpanter007. xanga.com." This blog was very difficult to find on the Internet. But Groth knew about it. It had been out there for a full year – created on August 18, 2011 – before I learned of it.

On September 11, 2012, Groth had a TV interview at 3 PM Pacific Time with Channel 2 in Reno. The topic of the 15-minute segment was her recent retirement announcement. At 4:36 PM Pacific time, the two anonymous emails were sent to my employer, specifically stating the intent to interfere with my employment. From the proximity of the interview with the send time of the bitter emails, I assumed she was upset about losing her position and blamed me. The venom she had for me for so many years was reinvigorated, compelling her to strike out again.

The false accusations contained in the emails were undeniably initiated by Groth since I do not know any of her family members. But Groth's animosity toward me over the loss of her career was misplaced. If she took an honest look in the mirror at herself, she would be forced to admit that it was her own behavior and that of her former golf coach Rich Merritt that ended her career as an AD.

I had moved to Nevada to build a high caliber NCAA Division I soccer program at the university. I delivered on my end, going about my work in an honest manner. For my efforts, I found myself in an endless struggle to escape a university administration immersed in a culture of retaliation and an avalanche of lies.

*   *   *

In the summer of 2011, while I was living far away from Nevada, I received a phone call from a friend who asked me if I was sitting down. He told me he had a friend who I didn't know who wanted to speak with me. His friend – who I will call George to protect his identity – took the phone and proceeded to share with me that he was a regular bettor at the sports books in Reno. He said that he witnessed who he believed to be Cary Groth placing bets on several occasions at two of the sports books that he frequented in 2010-11. George confirmed her identity with an online photo and added that she often wore Nevada Wolf Pack gear when she came in – which he said was as much as three times a week during the college basketball season. There were other witnesses including several employees at one of the casinos who also were aware of her betting activities. Because my case was still ongoing at the time, we notified General Counsel Dugan that Groth was alleged by witnesses to have been engaging in the very acts that she tried to cover up for golf coach Rich Merritt. What made this accusation even more troubling was that the university was on NCAA probation at the time due to the Rich Merritt fallout so any further violations during this period would have been very costly for the university.

While Dugan responded within hours demanding that we turn over any evidence we had, it took Groth's personal attorney John Arrascada *eleven days* to offer a denial of these very serious allegations. He stated that Groth and her sister have a "very similar resemblance and have often been mistaken for one another." He went on to say that "Groth's sister enjoys *occasional wagering on NFL games* and has every right to wager on sporting events." It is true that Groth and her sister share a strong resemblance and that her sister has every right to wager on sporting events – like every other citizen who is not subject to the NCAA's governing rules. But three different videos that I watched of this person who looked just like Cary Groth – and I knew her well – showed her placing bets on several *college* football games. The videos contradicted Arrascada's statement that it was NFL games that Groth's sister was betting on. In one video alone she placed bets on Boise State, Wisconsin, and a handful of other college teams. In another video she bet on a Tuesday night Northern Illinois University football game. Groth had previously been the AD at NIU and her sister was a former tennis coach there. On one evening during the college basketball season, the woman (Groth or her sister) asked George whether she should pick Nevada or Fresno State in that evening's basketball game. George said he told her that she should pick Fresno.

If Groth gave her sister insider knowledge on Nevada basketball to assist in her betting activities, Groth would be in violation of NCAA regulations. If Groth herself was doing the wagering it would have a significant and deleterious impact on both Groth and the university.

While I cannot be certain if the woman in the video was Groth or her sister, it did take Arrascada eleven days to address the allegations about his client with a response that was not truthful. If it really was Groth's sister and Groth had no involvement whatsoever, why lie? Four employees at one of the sports books in question witnessed this woman – who they believed to be the athletic director at Nevada – betting on a large number of occasions over a lengthy period of time. One of the employees said that the person wore clothing identifying her as the athletic director. Another employee was heard saying to the woman – "I saw you on TV last week". Groth, not her sister, had been on TV the week before. The woman just nodded her head in apparent ascension and prepared to place her bets. She didn't deny being the woman on TV.

In damage control mode, the university notified the NCAA of the allegations and declared that the woman placing bets was Groth's sister. That would eventually trigger a meeting between the NCAA enforcement staff and me. I was already skeptical of their investigative efforts in matters involving Nevada after their treatment of Groth in the previous investigation. My skepticism was confirmed when, after watching the videos, one investigator asked me "who in media knows about this?" One year later, in January 2013, the employees who alleged to have witnessed who they believed was Groth sports wagering said that neither they nor their employer had ever been contacted by the NCAA about this matter. The employees also said that since the time Dugan was first notified of the allegations of Groth's sports wagering in the fall of 2011, neither Groth nor her sister had been seen wagering in their sports book again.

*　　*　　*

In April 2011, then-UNR President Milton Glick died of a massive stroke. Marc Johnson was formally announced as his successor on April 20, 2012. Johnson had served as provost and executive vice president under Glick from 2008-2011. While Johnson arrived at Nevada after I left there, I do know that he had researched my situation and was well-versed on the retaliatory actions of Groth, Dugan, and others.

In August 2012, Cary Groth publicly announced her retirement after failing to receive a contract extension from Johnson. Her existing contract was set to expire in June 2013 – her last day in office was April 16, 2013. Despite Johnson's knowledge of Groth's unethical behavior as head of the university's department of athletics, he continued her employment for another year. According to Groth's contract, she could have been terminated for cause for:

> Any conduct of Employee in violation of any criminal statute of moral turpitude; Any behavior of Employee that brings Employee into public disrepute, contempt, scandal ridicule or any behavior that is unfavorable to the reputation or ethical standards of the University of Nevada, Reno.

Under these provisions, Johnson certainly had permission to terminate her contract immediately and without cost to the university. Instead he allowed her to continue to collect a salary at taxpayer expense for an additional year; evidence that the welfare of the student-athletes and the reputation of the university were secondary to protecting the retaliatory administration under Johnson as well.

In 2011, UNR General Counsel Mary Dugan was considered for a federal magistrate judgeship in Nevada but, according to a person with direct knowledge of the process, after the committee learned of her dubious activities as UNR General Counsel she failed to receive the appointment. Mary Dugan continues to be employed at the school under Johnson.

In early 2013, a letter was sent to Nevada's Governor, Attorney General, NSHE's Chancellor, members of its Board of Regents, several members of the UNR administration, and the heads of seven law enforcement agencies throughout Nevada. The letter was cc'd to the

Reno Gazette Journal and the *Las Vegas Sun* newspapers. The author of the letter urged for assistance with the ongoing situation at the UNR Police Department. Specifically, it asked that NSHE Chancellor Daniel Klaich and UNR President Marc Johnson take action. The author said this was the second such letter that had been sent seeking their help. The following excerpts from the letter indicate that the environment that existed under former President Milton Glick remains alive and well under Marc Johnson:

> How long will this once highly respected University and upper management allow Adam Garcia (Chief of Police) and Mary Dugan (General Counsel) to destroy people's lives, their livelihoods, and careers? The "black eye" on this University is slowly but surely getting exposed by these corrupt individuals that you continue to protect and keep in power . . . .
>
> The UNR Police Department has lost many good officers because of Garcia's pattern of lying, manipulating and abusing his power, along with the help of Dugan. This police department is in disarray, and the officers feel there is no hope for their future as police officers unless immediate actions are taken . . . .
>
> [Garcia] has tainted all of the camaraderie between the officers and what it meant to come to work and to try to do our job the very best that we could, unfortunately we, as police officers, now live in fear, we can hardly focus on the crime that is occurring in our jurisdiction because we focus so much on Garcia and his administration, and the fear of being disciplined and/or terminated . . . .
>
> I would love to place my signature on this paper, but I live in "FEAR" of Garcia not as an individual, but of losing my job or opening myself up for more retaliation that the University has allowed him to pursue thus far.
>
> Chief Garcia remains employed at the university.

* * *

I could have walked away and handed over my career to an unscrupulous AD or I could choose to fight for my reputation and my future. For those who wonder why I continued to pursue a legal remedy after being thwarted time and time again, I have some questions you might want to consider should you ever find yourself in a similar position.

- o Would you have looked the other way knowing that a colleague was going to bring down your program or your company?
- o Would you have stood up for your athletes or employees if they were being treated unfairly?
- o Would you have walked away from a possible legal remedy in the millions of dollars when you had mounds of evidence – including direct admissions of retaliation – to support your case?
- o Would you have abandoned the career you love without a fight?

I believed the justice system would work and treat me fairly. But no matter the ultimate outcome of my pursuit for justice, I feel satisfaction for standing up to injustice.

AFTERWORD

"If you are to build anything in this life, you can talk about loyalty, honesty, trust, all that – it comes down to truth. If you base everything on the truth and doing the right thing everything else is secondary."

~ Mike Pressler

In today's instant news / Twitter world, we all need to make decisions based on the assumption that the whole truth will eventually emerge. I did not want to write this book. But the actions of others gave me no choice. And it is by their own actions that the truth has finally emerged.

Over the past few years I have met and spoken with several AD's and senior administrators who have offered their support. They assured me that I did, not only the right thing, but what I was obligated to do under the NCAA's governing rules.

Since I left Nevada I have had the opportunity to work with nearly 1,000 soccer players who are enthusiastic and full of life. Seeing the world through their bright and innocent eyes gives one a sense of renewal and hope for the future. Although my experience in Nevada wasn't a pleasant one, I learned a lot and most importantly I found an inner strength and I survived to find myself in a better place.

I chose the path of most resistance. I could have walked away and taken the easy way out but that's not my nature. I'm a coach who always taught my athletes 'to be fighters and to play until the final whistle.' I couldn't ask less of myself.

I look forward to returning to a university campus and coaching student-athletes again in the near future.

In the meantime, in the Fall of 2013, I was asked to return to my high school – Mounds View – to lead their girls soccer program. We finished the season ranked #1 in the State in the final coaches poll after rattling off an 18-0 record. We outscored our opponents 61-5 as we went on to win the schools first-ever Suburban East Conference Championship and qualify for the State Tournament. It was the best season in the history of the Mounds View girls soccer program. The brilliant play of our wonderfully talented players led me to be named both "Conference Coach of the Year" and "Section Coach of the Year." But most importantly, the experience made me whole again.

With the completion of this book I have finally found my way out of the rabbit hole.

BIBLIOGRAPHY

Bills, Bronson D. "A Penny for the Court's Thoughts? The High Price of Judicial Elections." *Northwestern Journal of Law & Social Policy, Winter 2008, Volume 3, Issue 1, Article 2*

Dodd, Dennis. "Neuheisel gambles with his future by betting on hoops." *CBSSports.com,* June 5, 2003

Goodman, Michael J. and Rempel, William C. "In Las Vegas, They're Playing with a Stacked Judicial Deck." *Los Angeles Times*, June 8, 2006

Hoover, John E. "NCAA officials begin investigating Tulsa AD's gambling." *Tulsa World*, December 4, 2012

Katz, Andy. "Myck Kabongo's Ban Reduced", *ESPN*, December 23, 2012

Maimon, Alan. "Saitta nets a low tally on judge survey." *Las Vegas Review Journal,* May 19, 2008

McDonnell, Pat. "Distinguished Geography Professor Chris Exline Dies." *NevadaNews*, April 13, 2006

Miille, Margaret Ann. "Some lawyers perceive judicial bias." *Las Vegas Review Journal*, May 22, 2008

Miille, Margaret Ann. "Some lawyers perceive judicial bias." *Las Vegas Review Journal*, Posted May 22, 2008, Updated April 9, 2012

Miller, Steve. "Like Father, Like Son." *Inside Vegas*, September 27, 2004

Miller, Steve. "A Judge in Their Pocket." *Inside Vegas* (americanmafia.com), August 15, 2005

Miller, Steve. "Nevada Supreme Court Justice Nancy Saitta's mob associations may haunt her re-election bid." *Inside Vegas* (americanmafia.com), January 9, 2012

Morrison, Jane Ann. "Lying on resumes to make yourself look good can get ugly pretty fast." *reviewjournal.com*, Posted November 12, 2007, Updated April 9, 2012

Mullen, Jr., Frank X. "University of Nevada's Camera Network Raises Fear." *Reno-Gazette-Journal*, December 20, 2011

NCAA. "The Ohio State University Public Infractions Report." *NCAA Committee on Infractions*, December 20, 2011

NCAA. "The University of Nevada, Reno, Public Infractions Report." *NCAA Committee on Infractions*, March 18, 2010

NCAA. "The University of Tennessee Public Infractions Report." *NCAA Committee on Infractions*, August 24. 2011

Nevada Association of Public Safety Officers, The. "Police Officers and the Community Fight Back Against Criminal Acts Committed by University of Nevada Reno Officials." *Press Release*, October 19, 2009. Retrieved from www.examiner.com/article/criminal-acts-alleged-at-the-university-of-nevada-reno

Oxarart, Scott. "Investigation Info Could Come Soon." *Nevada Sagebrush*, March 11, 2008

Skolnik, Sam. "Judge Lands in Middle of Feud." *Las-Vegas Sun*, July 21, 2006

Stitt, Grant (chair) "Report of the Ad-Hoc Committee on Faculty Morale to the Faculty Senate." April 17, 2005

Watkins, Calvin. "Bryant Ineligible for Rest of Season." *ESPN,* November 5, 2009

Made in the USA
Las Vegas, NV
29 August 2022